Learn Latin In 7 DAYS!

The Ultimate Crash Course to Learning the Basics of the Latin Language in No Time

By Dagny Taggart

Disclaimer

The information provided in this book is designed to provide helpful information on the subjects discussed. The author's books are only meant to provide the reader with the basics knowledge of a certain language, without any warranties regarding whether the student will, or will not, be able to incorporate and apply all the information provided. Although the writer will make her best effort share her insights, language learning is a difficult task, and each person needs a different timeframe to fully incorporate a new language. This book, nor any of the author's books constitute a promise that the reader will learn a certain language within a certain timeframe.

Table of Contents

Preview Of "Learn Greek In 7 DAYS! - The Ultimate Crash Course To Learn The Basics of the Greek Language In No Time"

About the Author

Dedicated to those who love going beyond their own frontiers.

Keep on traveling,

Dagny Taggart

Introduction

Salvete Omnes!

Latin has a way of sneaking up on one in the most common places. When was the last time you took a minute to study the back of a dollar bill? Or read your state motto? Or heard a Latin phrase in a television show or in a movie? Or perhaps there is a Latin phrase in your favorite novel? Maybe there was a legal term in your history textbook. Latin is everywhere.

Latin has a long history as it dates all the way back to the Roman Empire, one of the most powerful and influential ancient civilizations in our recorded history. The Romans were a powerful and dynamic people that strove for excellence and preeminence among their peers and among other nations. As a result they left an enduring legacy that still influences the world today.

One of the most amazing things about language is the power it has to communicate our thoughts and ideas. It is even more amazing that we are able to peer into the past through the window of language. We can learn about what those before us said, did, and thought about. I sometimes find it startling how much we still have in common with people from the past. The Roman world can feel so much like ours at times with a vast, complicated, and often frustrating political system. The huge emphasis on entertainment and leisure with enthusiasts that were just as passionate as world cup followers today.

One of the most rewarding things about studying Latin is that just a little bit can give you a lot of mileage. Studying law, medicine, history, science, or literature will bring you into contact with many Latin phrases. Plus, Latin has hardly retreated from our popular culture. The famous Harry Potter series has the first two books translated into Latin, *Harrius Potter et Philosophi Lapis* and *Harrius Potter et Camera Secretorum.* Many other classic children's books are also translated into Latin editions. Many movies and TV series have episodes with Latin in them. In addition, studying Latin can help improve your vocabulary as many English words are derived from its roots. It will also bring you into contact with some of the most enduring thoughts and perspectives in all of human history.

Why You Can't Afford Not to Learn Latin (Yes, I'm Serious!)

Many people are skeptical about studying Latin and wonder how much worth it will be to learn a language that is hardly spoken anymore in the modern world. Yet Latin is very useful language to acquire even in the modern world. Here are 7 reasons why Latin should be a language that you should start studying today.

1. I suppose we'll start with the most idealistic reason it is necessary to study Latin. The study of Latin helps us to preserve ancient history. Roman history is interesting, Roman history is fun, and it is also important. The fact of the matter is that studying ancient humans tells us a lot about humanity and about ourselves. Having this knowledge allows us to create a better world for everyone. Many modern day governments rely on traditions and political concepts valued in the Roman Republic. Because we have learned from strengths and flaws of the Roman Republic we are able to sustain successful democracies today.

2. Latin is the original language of many famous works of literature. Not all literature is good because it is old. But what is good usually gets preserved. At least we hope. That is why what literature we have left from ancient Rome is often of a high standard of skill and style. Studying this high quality literature is helpful not only for cultural enrichment but to study the stylistic qualities that influenced literature for centuries afterward. The content of Roman literature helps the student become familiar with historical tropes, themes, and points of view. In addition, reading ancient books gives the student background knowledge with which to analyze other works of literature. The stylistic choices of authors teach students to recognize figures of speech and meter written by masters of these art forms. This increases recognition and appreciation of these skills in their own languages. This leads to increased ease of imitating these skills when attempting their own writing.

3. Reading these famous works of art in their original language is worth it. Translations are never perfect. There are simply ways of thinking and talking that are native to the Latin language that does not transfer over to English. Hearing/reading Latin in the original is an experience that cannot be recreated with a translation. The beauty of

Latin is found in its unique way to convey ideas concisely and with emphasis in the most surprising of places. The beauty of Latin is found in the layers of phrases leading up to a crescendo of understanding. The beauty of learning in any language is thinking about the world from a different point of view than your own.

4. As a corollary to the importance of reading works of art in their original language. There are many areas of expertise that require interpretation of ancient primary sources. Since Latin was the universal language of the western world for such a long period of time many important documents are written in Latin. This includes important religious books (vulgate bible), historical records, foundational legal documents (magna carta), scientific discoveries, medical knowledge, and numerous other documents that hold important information. The ability to access these primary sources in the original is a necessity for being considered a credible professional in many academic fields.

5. Latin was and still is a universal language in academics. Many scientific discoveries of plants and animals are christened with Latin names. Cartographers and mapmakers labeled the world in Latin. This is because for so long Latin was the universal language by which Europeans communicated with one another and with the church. It was considered an essential part of all educational pursuits. This reliance on Latin gives the advantage of many countries being able to use scientific discoveries. Issac Asimov argues that this use of Latin encouraged scientific cooperation from many different countries and helped to spur scientific progress.

6. Studying Latin helps you learn your own language. Many educators praise the effect of learning a second language because it helps you to understand your own language. This is true. Learning a different language often helps the student gain knowledge of parts of speech, verb tenses, and other important aspects of their own language. Understanding these grammar principals helps students to communicate with more clarity and precision. For example, English used to have cases, but over time they dropped from the language. Yet, there is still evidence of this in our language. Ever wonder about the difference between who and whom, he and him, I and me? Our personal pronouns still show the tradition of cases. Who, he, and I

are all meant to be subjects of a verb or in nominative case. Whom, him, and me are all objects or accusative case. The added advantage of learning Latin is that it helps students learn the vocabulary of their own language because so many words are derived from it.

7. The fact that Latin helps students improve their English language skills has made the language well known for increasing test scores. Many Latin promotion materials point out that over 90% of words over two syllables have Latin roots. In addition, Dictionary.com says that 90% of science and technology vocabulary are influenced by Latin. So learning Latin helps students excel on SAT and GRE and other word based tests. Learning Latin also decreases the time one must study for these test because they have already acquired the background knowledge needed to pass.

How Latin Is Different From Modern Languages

I had a professor in college once that remarked upon how interesting it is that sound of the ancient human voice is lost to us. Think about how different our world is today. We have access to audio, image, and video files of all the greatest leaders in modern history. Yet, we will never hear the text of the poetic *Aenied* performed by a native speaker. The voice of Cicero, the ancient world's most renowned orator, is beyond our reach.

So we cannot know everything about Latin with exact precision. We may look to the writings we have to look for answers to grammatical or historical questions, but we often find them lacking. We can't sit down with a Roman and ask them how things were really said or done. So, we have to do our best with the writings and clues that we have. The more that time moves on the further we move away from Roman history and culture.

Latin is rarely spoken as a living language anymore and it wasn't that long ago that it was considered important. When the Catholic Church stopped doing mass in Latin there was much less emphasis placed on speaking Latin. So many education programs focused on their students reading Latin so that students might use it to read classical, medieval, and other historical works. The language is still very useful in this context. Some Latin teachers will insist on students learning the finer nuances of Latin pronunciation and oration, but that is not the goal of this text. I'll highlight some important alphabetical differences for reference sake but not all.

Latin is the mother of many of the romance languages: Spanish, Italian, Portuguese, and French. These languages all evolved from a vulgar Latin that was very different from Classical Latin. The tendency moved toward simplifying the highly inflected grammatical forms until languages no longer declined nouns but still kept their gender.

However, Latin never had articles like many romance languages do. Articles like "the" and "a" must be put in by a translator in the places that they feel most natural and make the most sense to the modern English speaker or reader.

Memorization is important with any language, but particularly so with Latin. Then gender of nouns and their declensions must be memorized. The verbs have four principal parts that must be memorized also in order to conjugate them in all tenses. It is helpful to repeat aloud the vocabulary entries and write them down. It is helpful to remember words by identifying derivatives. As a student I was a fan of flashcards.

With the study of any language one must be willing to make mistakes. It is only by correcting our mistakes over and over that we are able to learn and to commit to memory the correct way to do things. Do not be too harsh on yourself as you learn a language. It is a difficult process. Remember that every child learning their native language must also make a lot of mistakes to learn how to speak, read, and write in their native tongue. With persistence and effort you can learn a good amount of the Latin language.

SECTION ONE:
THE BASICS

Chapter 1
Pronunciation and Alphabet

One of the easy things for English students of Latin is the fact that the Roman alphabet is—with few exceptions—the same. This gives a distinct advantage over someone beginning to study a language with a wholly foreign alphabet.

The Roman alphabet did not have the letter **j** or **w.** This claim may raise several eyebrows. What about *Julius* *Caesar*? The **j** sound was made with the combination of two letters **i** and **u.** Therefore, we would have **Iulius** Caesar.

The letter **v** is also a little tricky. The symbol **v** stood for the consonant sound **w** and the vowel sound **u**. It wasn't until much later that the curved **u** was differentiated from the **v.**   To avoid confusion many modern day texts are edited to use the curved **u** when the vowel sound is necessary.

Vowel sounds are either long or short.

Long	Short
a as in Father	**a** as in art
e as in they	**e** as in pet
i as in machine	**i** as in pin
o as in no	**o** as in hot
u as in tube	**u** as in put

Latin also has six diphthongs. A diphthong is the combination of two vowels in a row and they make a specific sound.

ae as in aisle
au as in ou in house
ei as in reign
eu as in e+u pronounced together as if a single syllable
ui as in u+i pronounced together as if a single syllable
oe as in oi in oil

Consonants:

c is always pronounced hard as in can.
g is always pronounced hard as in get.

q is always followed by a u and thus has a kw sound.
r is trilled as it often is in Spanish.
v is pronounced as our w.
x is pronounced as ks

Double consonants were always pronounced as two separate consonants. They were not blended together as they often are in English. Pulcherrima for example is pulcher—rima.

Salve!	Hello!
Quid est nomen tibi?	What is your name?
Nomen mihi est _____.	My name is _____.
Quid agis?	How are you?
Optime!	Great!
Pessime!	Terrible!
Bene!	Good
Satis bene	Okay
Non bene	Not well
Et, tu?	And you?
Vale!	Goodbye!
gratias ago tibi	Thank you
amabo te	Please
me paenitet	Sorry
Ignosce mihi	excuse me
Bene factum!	Good job!
Benigne	No thank you
Bonam fortunam!	Good luck!

Practice: Translate the following into English

Salve!-->
Quid est nomen tibi? Nomen mihi est Julia.-->
Nomen mihi est Livia. -->
Quid agis, Livia?-->
Pessime!-->
Me paenitet. Bonam fortunam!-->
Gratias ago tibi. Vale!-->

Translation answers

Hello!
What is your name? My name is Julia.
My name is Livia.
How are you, Livia?
Terrible!

I'm sorry. Good Luck!
Thank you. Good bye.

Chapter 4
Numbers and Colors

Numbers 1-10

Unus-a-um	One	I
Duo, duae, duo	Two	II
Tres, tria	Three	III
Quattor	Four	IV
Quinque	Five	V
Sex	Six	VI
Septem	Seven	VII
Octem	Eight	VIII
Novem	Nine	IX
Decem	Ten	X

Numbers 11-20

Undecim	Eleven	XI
Duodecim	Twelve	XII
Tredecim	Thirteen	XIII
Quattordecim	Fourteen	XIV
Quindecim	Fifteen	XV
Sedecim	Sixteen	XVI
Septendecim	Seventeen	XVII
Duodeviginti	Eighteen	XVIII
Undeviginti	Nineteen	XIX
Viginti	Twenty	XX

Note: notice that eighteen and nineteen break the pattern. Duo-de-viginiti-->two from twenty or eighteen. Un-de-viginti--> one from twenty or nineteen.

Numbers 20-100

Viginti unus or unus et viginti	Twenty one	XXI
Triginta	Thirty	XXX
Quadraginta	Forty	XL
Quinquaginta	Fifty	L

Sexaginta	Sixty	LX
Septuaginta	Seventy	LXX
Octoginta	Eighty	LXXX
Nonaginta	Ninety	XC
Centum	one hundred	C

Note: There are two ways to write numbers from this point. **Viginti unus, viginti duo, viginti tres** just as in English. The other way is to use et—**viginti et unus viginti et duo, viginti et tres**.

Number 100-1000

Ducenti	Two hundred	CC
Trecenti	Three hundred	CCC
Quadringenti	Four hundred	CD
Quingenti	Five hundred	D
Sescenti	Six hundred	DC
Septingenti	Seven hundred	DCC
Octingenti	Eight hundred	DCCC
Nongenti	Nine hundred	CM
Mille	Thousand	M
Duo milia	Two thousand	MM

Colors

Rufus	Red
Flavus	Yellow
Venetus	Blue
Viridis	Green
Purpureus	Purple
Aurantius	Orange
Niger	Black
Albus	White

Months

Ianuarius	January
Februarius	February
Martius	March
Aprilis	April
Maius	May
Junius	June
Julius (quintilis)	July
Augustus (sextilis)	August
September	September
October	October
November	November
December	December

Originally, the Roman calendar had only ten months. Shown by the fact that the last four months of the year are known as the seventh, eighth, ninth, and tenth. Then January and February were added to the beginning of the calendar year. March used to be the first month of the Roman year. January is named in honor of the god Janus. February is most likely named in honor of the Roman holiday Februa. Martius is named in honor of the god of war, Mars. April in honor of Fortuna Virilis, who is closely linked with Venus. Maius in honor of the goddess Maia. Junius in honor of the goddess Juno. Late in the Roman Empire Augustus Caesar named the month Quintilis in honor of his uncle Julius Caesar. Years later Sextilis was finally named in honor of Augustus himself.

Days of the week

dies Solis	Sunday
dies Lunae	Monday
dies Martis	Tuesday
dies Mercurii	Wednesday
dies Jovis	Thursday
dies Veneris	Friday
dies Saturni	Saturday

Quid die Lunae facis? ---> What do you do on Monday?

Laboro ---> I work

Scholam obeo ---> I go to school.

Quid die Saturni facis? ---> What do you do on Saturday?

Ludo-->I play

Dormio--> I sleep

Hour according to the Romans

The Romans reckoned time differently than we do. The sun rising marked the beginning of the first hour. In the below 6:00 am is the example for when the day begins but of course this would have fluctuated depending on the time of year and location. The Romans did split the day into twelve hour increments and did the same with the evening hours. **Meridies** is noon, **Media Nox** is midnight.

6:00 am	hora prima	First hour
7:00 am	hora secunda	Second hour
8:00 am	hora tertia	Third hour
9:00 am	hora quarta	Forth hour
10:00 am	hora quinta	Fifth hour
11:00 am	hora sexta	Sixth hour
12:00 pm	hora septima	Seventh hour
1:00 pm	hora octava	Eighth hour
2:00 pm	hora nona	Ninth hour
3:00 pm	hora decima	Tenth hour
4:00 pm	hora undecima	Eleventh hour
5:00 pm	hora duodecima	Twelfth hour

Quota hora excites? --> At what hour do you wake up?

Hora prima--> The first hour.

Quota hora dorimis?--> At what hour do you sleep?

Hora duodecima --> the twelfth hour.

Quota hora prandium sumis? --> At what our do you eat lunch?

Hora septima or **Meridies**--> The seventh hour or midday.

The year according to the Romans

The years were originally kept track of by naming them by the two roman consuls that served that year. In 59 B.C. Julius Caesar was elected as consul with a man named Bibulus. Caesar worked hard to further his own aims and those of his political allies often ignoring his co-consul Bibulus. This led to many people in the senate making the joke that it was the consulship of Julius and Caesar.

Eventually, it became common to reckon the time from the founding of the city, which is calculated by scholars to be around B.C. 753. So to make Roman dates correspond with our current calendar we must subtract the year of the city from 754.

Yes or no?

Something odd about Latin is that there really is no way to say yes. There are ways to convey the idea of yes, of course, but there is no word for word translation for the word yes. Romans used several ways to convey the idea of agreement with several adverbs.

Ita est	Thus, so
Certe	Of course
Etiam	Even, certainly

While the above phrases work, the most appropriate way to answer yes in Latin is to reaffirm the main verb of the question.

actorem laudat?--> does he praise the actor?

actorem Laudat.--> he praises the actor.

Pecuniam capis?--> do you take the money?

Capio--> I take.

Saying no is *much* simpler:

Non	No
Minime	Not at all
Minime vero!	Certainly not!

Some notes about questions:

There was more than one way for the Romans to ask questions. The most direct was to use an interrogative word and the verb.

Another was to add the enclitic –**ne** to the end of the first work of the question. The presence of –**ne** would indicated to the hearer and reader that the phrase was a question.

Yet, Romans could go one step further and indicate what answer they expected. If the question was supposed to have a yes answer they would use the introductory word **nonne**.

If the expected answer was supposed to be no, the introductory word would be **num**.

Quis	Who?
Quid	What?
Ubi	Where?
Quot	How many?
Quotiens	How often?
Cur	Why?
Quantus	How great?
Quomodo	How?

Examples:

Quid bibis?--> what do you drink?

Ubi habitas?-->where do you live?

Comprehendisne libros?--> Do you understand the books?

pugnasne leonem aut ursam?--> Do your fight lions or bears?

Nonne Carmen cantas?--> You sing the song, don't you?

Num Carmen cantas?--> You don't sing that song, do you?

Conjunctions:

Et	And
Atque or ac	And, and also
-que	And
At	But
Sed	But
Aut	Or
Vel	Or
-Ve	Or

Neque or nec	And not
Et....et	Both...and
Atque....atque	Both...and
Aut...aut	Either...or
Nec...nec...	Neither....nor

Et is probably familiar to many people from the famous line, **"et tu, Brute?"** Encountered by most students while reading Shakespeare's play *Julius Caesar*. It is also part of the oft used abbreviation etc. or **et cetera**—and other things. **Et** is also the inspiration for the ampersand (e.g. &).

Another note on the conjunctions **–que** and **–ve.** They are what are called enclitics or words that attach themselves to the end of words. When a -**que** or- **ve** is attached to the end of a word it means that it is linking it to the word before it. The quickest way to make this all clear is to give examples.

Milites et poetae—soldiers and poets

mater et pater filiusque--> Mother and father and son

arma virumque--> arms and a man

panem vinumque --> bread and wine

puer puellave--> boy or girl

nox diesve--> night or day

Useful adverbs

Hodie	Today
Semper	Always
Cras	Tomorrow
Nunc	Now
Statim	Immediately
Etiam	Also, besides
Tarde	Slow
Velocriter	Quickly
Saepe	Often
Numquam	Never

Prepositions

Latin Preposition are small and sometimes annoying words because they are easy to mix up, yet they are some of the most useful Latin words to know. They are often the building blocks for many verbs in Latin. Often a preposition is added on to a common Latin verb to give it a new sense or meaning.

For example:

Venio, venire—to come

Invenio, invenire—to find

Advenio, advenire—to arrive

In addition to being helpful building blocks in Latin vocabulary, they are extremely helpful to know when trying to improve English vocabulary. A decent amount of English words also use these words as prefixes. Knowing these words can take you a long way in getting a sense of what words mean even if you don't know their precise definition.

All prepositions take nouns as their objects. In Latin prepositions can take two cases either ablative or accusative. In general, accusative case has a sense of motion to it, while the ablative case is stationary. Some prepositions can take both the ablative and accusative case. When this happens the case often implies a different sense. For example: **in** plus the accusative means into, while **in** plus the ablative means in.

a/ab	By, from	Ablative
Ad	To, toward	Accusative
Ante	Before	Accusative
Circum	Around	Accusative
Contra	Against	accusative
Cum	With	Ablative
De	Down from, concerning	Ablative
e/ex	Out of	Ablative
Extra	Outside of	Accusative

In	Into/onto	accusative
In	In/ on	ablative
Inter	Between	Accusative
Intra	Within	accusative
Per	Through, because of	Ablative
Propter	Because of, on account of	Accusative
Pro	Before, on behalf of	ablative
Prae	Before, in front of	Ablative
Post	After, behind	accusative
Sub	under	Accusative or ablative
Sine	Without	Ablative
Super	Above	Accusative or ablative
Trans	across	Accusative
Ob	On account of	accusative

SECTION TWO
GRAMMAR

Chapter 7
Two Irregular Verbs

The first irregular verb that I want to explain is **sum, esse**-to be. The two be verb is irregular and so the forms simple have to be memorized.

Sum	I am
Es	You are
Est	He/she/it is
Sumus	We are
Estis	You all are
Sunt	They are

Examples:

Sum puella-->.I am a girl.
Puer est.--> He is a boy
Actores sunt-->They are actors.
Mater est.--> She is a Mother.
Felix es.-->   You are happy.

The second Latin verb to review is possum, posse. It is another irregular verb whose forms must be memorized.

Possum	I can
Potes	You can
Potest	He/she/it can
Possumus	We can
Potestis	You all can
Possunt	They can

Translate the following:

Sum

Possunt

Estis

Sunt

Puella es

Actores sumus

Pater est

Potestis

Milites sunt

Sunt poetae

Potes

Answers:

I am

They can

You all are

You are a girl

We are actors

He is a father

They all can

They are soldiers

They are poets

You can

Chapter 8
Nouns Declensions 1-5

In the beginning of my Latin studies I would try to look up a word in a Latin dictionary only to be perplexed by the fact that there were two versions of the word I was looking up. If you have ever had this baffling experience let me enlighten you as to why each word has two forms in the typical Latin dictionary. Nouns are split up into families called **declensions**, and each declension has specific characteristics and traits. Each declension has six **cases**: nominative, accusative, dative, genitive, ablative, and vocative.

In order for the student to know in which declension each word belongs they are listed in first the nominative case and then the genitive case. First declension words are listed as **puella, puellae** (girl). Second declension as **hortus, horti.**(garden) Third declension as **rex, regis** (king). The fourth declension as **cornus, cornus** (horn). The fifth declension as **res, rei** (thing).

The fact that Latin words have cases explains why several English words imported from Latin have puzzling plurals. For example: The plural of alumnus is alumni, syllabus is syllabi, antenna is antennae, formula is formulae, millennium is millennia, larva is larvae, appendix is appendices. However, octopi is often falsely used as a plural for octopus. The word octopus passed into English from Greek so octopuses is the correct plural.

Practice

1. Identify the declension of Puer, pueri
2. Identify the declension of Mater, Matris
3. Identify the declension of Nauta, Nautae
4. Identify the declension of Pater, Patris
5. Identify the declension of porta, portae
6. Identify the declension of populus, populi

Answers:

1. second
2. third
3. first
4. third

5. first
6. second

The First Declension

The first declension is made up primarily of feminine nouns. There are several exceptions to this rule. Words like *poeta-ae* (poet), *nauta-ae*(sailor), and *agricola-ae*(farmer) are part of the first declension, but they are masculine. An easy way to remember this is that a majority of sailors, poets, and farmers were male (and therefore masculine) in the ancient world.

To decline a noun you simple take off the genitive ending to find the stem and add the noun endings in the chart below.

Singular	Plural
Nom **a**	**ae**
Gen **ae**	**arum**
Acc **am**	**as**
Dat **ae**	**is**
Abl **a**	**Is**
Voc **a**	**ae**

Example of puella-ae(girl) declined.

Puella	Puellae
Puellae	Puellarum
Puellam	Puellas
Puellae	Puellis
Puella	Puellis
Puella	Puella

The Second Declension

The second declension is made up primarily of masculine nouns. Feminine gendered nouns in the second declension are very rare and are usually plants, gemstones or proper names. In addition to masculine nouns finding neuter nouns is very common. A neuter noun is easy to spot because it will have –**um** nominative, for example— **cubiculum, cubiculi**. These neuter nouns have different plural endings. A normal masculine noun has –**us** endings.

Singular	**Plural**

Nom **us** or **um** if neuter noun	**i** or **a** if neuter noun
Gen **i**	**orum**
Acc **um**	**os or a** if nuetuer noun
Dat **o**	**is**
Abl **o**	**is**
Voc **e**	**I**

Example of masculine second declension noun—hortus, horti(garden).

Hortus	Horti
Horti	Hororum
Hortum	Hortos
Horto	Hortis
Horto	Hortis
Horte	Horti

Example of a neuter second declension noun-cubiculum, cubicula(bedroom)

Cubiculum	Cubicula
Cubiculi	Cubiculorum
Cubiculum	Cubicula
Cubiculo	Cubiculis
Cubiculo	Cubiculis
Cubicule	Cubicula

Practice: Identify these nouns as masculine or neuter

Dominus, Domini (master)

Bellum, Belli (war)

Gladius, Gladii (sword)

Sevus, servi (servant)

Imperium, imperii (power)

Discipulus, discipuli (student)

Scutum, scuti (shield)

Auxilium, auxilii (help)

Cibus, cibi (food)

Answers:

Masculine

Neuter

Masculine

Masculine

Neuter

Masculine

Neuter

Neuter

masculine

The Third Declension

The Third Declension is another "family" of nouns. You can recognize a third declension noun by the genitive singular ending **–is**.

The Third Declension is larger and more complicated than the first or second declension. First of all, it has lots of masculine, feminine, and neuter nouns of all types.

Second it has no standard nominative singular stem. In order to decline the word you must find the stem from the genitive singular. When you remove the **–is** you will have the stem. Then add the third declension endings to this base.

Examples:

Soror, Sororis

stem=soror

Pater, Patris

stem=Patr

Rex, Regis

stem=reg

Singular	Plural
Nom --	**es** or **a** if neuter
Gen **is**	**um**
Acc **em**	**es** or **a** if neuter
Dat **i**	**ibus**
Abl **e**	**ibus**
Voc --	**es**

Example of masculine third declension noun rex, regis (king) declined. Feminine gendered nouns follow the exact same pattern as masculine.

Rex	**Reges**
Regis	**Regum**
Regem	**Reges**
Regi	**Regibus**
Rege	**Regibus**
Rex	**Reges**

Example of neuter third declension noun Carmen, carmenis(song, poem) declined.

Carmen	**Carmina**
Carminis	**Carminum**
Carminem	**Carmina**
Carmini	**Carminibus**
Carmine	**Carminibus**
Carmen	**Carmina**

Practice: find the stems for these third declension nouns

Pax, Pacis (peace)

Mos, Moris (custom)

Labor, Laboris (work)

Corpus, coporis (body)

Civitas, civitatis (state)

Laus, laudis (praise)

Mercator, mercatoris (merchant)

Ratio, rationis (reason)

Panis, panis (bread)

Answers:

Pac

Mor

Labor

Copor

Civitat

Laud

Mercator

Ration

pan

The Fourth Declension

The fourth Declension is much simpler than the third declension. It has fewer nouns, the majority of them masculine. There are a very small number of feminine nouns domus (house) and Manus (hand) among them. There are also a small group of neuter nouns that always have a –u in the nominative stem.

Singular	Neuter endings	Plural	Neuter endings
Nom **us**	u	**us**	**ua**
Gen **us**	**us**	**uum**	**uum**
Acc **um**	u	**us**	**ua**
Dat **ui**	u	**ibus**	**ibus**
Abl **u**	u	**ibus**	**ibus**
Voc us	u		

Example of masculine fourth declension noun senatus, senatus (senate) declined.

Senatus	**Senatus**
Senatus	**Senatuum**
Senatum	**Senatus**
Senatui	**Senatibus**
Senatu	**Senatibus**
Senatus	**Senatus**

Example of neuter fourth declension noun genu, genus (knee) declined.

Genu	**Genua**
Genus	**Genuum**
Genu	**Genua**
Genu	**Genibus**
Genu	**Geniubs**
Genu	**Genua**

The Fifth Declension

The fifth declension is another small and simple declension. The nouns in this declension are all feminine except for the exception of Die, Diei (day).

Singular	Plural
Nom **es**	**es**
Gen **ei**	**erum**
Acc **em**	**es**
Dat **ei**	**ebus**
Abl **e**	**ebus**
Voc **es**	**Es**

Example feminine nouns res , rei (thing) declined.

Res	**Res**
Rei	**Rerum**
Rem	**Res**
Rei	**Rebus**
Re	**Rebus**
Res	**Res**

Res may look familiar to some people because the Romans called their state the **res publica**, or the public thing. This is where our word republic comes from. A republic is a form of government where power is shared.

Chapter 9
Using Nominative and Vocative Cases Properly

Each case signals to the reader the particular role of a word in the sentence. Nominative case determines the subject, accusative determines the object, dative determines the indirect object, and genitive determines possession (e.g. Maria's book). The Ablative case is the most complex of the six, and is often referred to as the adverbial case because it often modifies or limits verbs. **The ablative is used often with prepositions, but can also be used without prepositions.**

Nominative case indicates the subject of the sentence. The subject of the sentence is the person or thing completing the action of the verb.

Examples:

Puella rosam dat. --> The girl gives a rose.

Puella is the subject of the sentence because she is the one giving. Notice that **Puella** is in the nominative case.

Magister pueros laudat. --> The teacher praises the boys.

Magister is the person doing the action in the sentence—praising. So it is in the nominative case and the subject of the sentence.

The Nominative case is also used with simple sum, esse sentences as shown below.

Magister est iratus. --> The teacher is angry.

Sum fessus. --> I am tired.

Livia est Mater. --> Livia is a mother.

The vocative case is used when the writer/speaker is addressing someone directly.

O puella, deos lauda. --> Oh girl, praise the gods.

Domine, mihi ignosce.--> Master, forgive me.

Practice: Identify the case of the underlined word in the sentences below. Then translate.

<u>Dominus</u> panem dat.
<u>O Fortuna</u>, panem das.
<u>Discipule</u>, puellam lauda.
<u>Hortus</u> est pulcher.
<u>Poeta</u> carmina cantat.
<u>Puer</u> est iratus.
<u>Mater</u>, pueros laudat.
<u>Livia</u> est poeta.

Answers:

Nominative. The master gives bread.
Vocative. O Fortuna, you give bread.
Vocative. Student, praise the girl.
Nominative. The garden is beautiful.
Nominative. The poet sings songs.
Nominative. The boy is angry.
Vocative. Mother, praise the boys.
Nominative. Livia is a poet.

Chapter 10
Noun Adjective Agreement

As established above nouns in Latin have three aspects—gender, number, and case. In regards to gender nouns can be masculine, feminine, or neuter. Number refers to whether a noun is singular or plural. Lastly nouns have case endings: nominative, genitive, accusative, dative, ablative and vocative.

When nouns are paired up with adjectives the adjective must decline to agree with the noun it modifies in gender, number, and case. There are two groups of adjectives, those that decline like first and second declension nouns and those that decline like third declension nouns.

Examples of magnus-a-um

Puella magna	Puellae magnae
Puellae magnae	Puellarum magnarum
Puellam magnam	Puellas magnas
Puellae magnae	Puellis magnis
Puella magna	Puellis magnis

Hortus magnus	Horti magni
Horti magni	Hortorum magnorum
Hortum magnum	Hortos magnos
Horto magno	Hortis magnis
Horto magno	Hortis magnis

Note: While nouns and adjectives have to agree in gender, number and case they don't necessarily have to agree in declension. Below is an example of magnus-a-um modifying a third declension neuter noun.

Carmen magnum	Carmina magna
Carminis magni	Carmenum magnorum
Carminem magnum	Carmina magna
Carmini magno	Carminibus magnis
Carmine magno	Carminibus magnis

Third declension adjectives

Third declension adjectives work like their first and second declension counterparts but their endings differ in a few places from the typical third declension endings. Below is a chart of the adjective celer, celeris, celere (swift, quick). First, the vocabulary has three forms. The first for the masculine singular nominative(celer) and the second for the feminine singular nominative (celeris) and the third is for the neuter singular nominative (celere). The ablative singular turns into an -i instead of an -e. The plural neuter has an-ia ending. The genitive plural has a-ium ending.

Celer, celeris	Celere	Celeres	Celeria
Celeris	Celeris	Celerium	Celerium
Celerem	Celere	Celeres	Celeria
Celeri	Celeri	Celeribus	Celeribus
Celeri	Celeri	Celeribus	Celeribus

Examples:

Rex celer	Reges celeries
Regis celeris	Regum celerium
Regem celerem	Reges celeries
Regi celeri	Regibus celeribus
Rege celeri	Regibus celeribus
Rex celer	Reges celeribus

Carmen celer	Carmina celeria
Carminis celeris	Carminum celerium
Carminem celerem	Carmina celeria
Carmini celeri	Carminibus celeribus
Carmine celeri	Carminibus celeribus
Carmen celer	Carmina celeria

Puella celeris	Puellae celeries
Puellae celeris	Puellarum celerium
Puellam celerem	Puellas celeries
Puellae celeri	Puellis celeribus
Puella celeri	Puellis celeribus

Practice: match the noun with the appropriate adjective ending

Pacem magn___. (pax, pacis *f. peace)*

puellas celer__.

regibus magn__.

Cubiculum mang__.

Dominus mangn___.

Carmine celer__.

Puellas magn___.

Carminum celer__.

Horto magn__.

Answers:

Magnam

Celeres

magnis

mangnum

magnus

celeri

magnas

celerium

magno

10.1
Comparison of Adjectives

In the section above we learned the positive aspect of adjectives. Positive is a grammatical term that denotes the fact that the adjective is only applying to one thing. An adjective is called comparative if it compares two nouns to each other and superlative when there is more than two things to compare. To form a comparative adjective the formula is to take the stem of the word and add ior (mas&fem), ius(neuter), ioris (new genitive ending).

Superlative is the base plus issimus, issima, issimum.

Positive	Comparative	Superlative
Fortis-e (strong)	Fortior, ius	Fortissimus-a-um
Felix, felicis (happy)	Felicior, ius	Felicissimus-a-um
Iratus,a,um (angry)	Iratior, ius	Iratissimus-a-um
Callidus-a-um (clever)	Callidior, ius	Callidissimus-a-um
Tristis-e (sad)	Tristior, ius	Tristissimus, a, um

Note: When quam follows a comparative adjective it means than and serves as a conjunction to compare two nouns.

Examples:

Magister est iratus.--> the teacher is mad

Discipulus est iratius.--> The student is more angry

Mater discipuli est iratissima.--> The mother of the student is most angry.

Nauta est callidior quam miles.--> The sailor is more clever than the soldier.

Practice: Translate

Pueri sunt fortis.

Pueri sunt fortior.

Pueri sunt fortissimi.

Canis est felix.

Canis est felicior quam homo.

Servus est callidior quam dominus.

Puella est Felicissima.

Answers

The boys are strong.

The boys are stronger.

The boys are the strongest.

The dog is happy.

The dog is more happy than the man.

The slave is more clever than the master.

The girl is the most happy.

Irregular Adjectives

There are several adjectives that irregular superlative forms. The first are adjectives ending in **–lis** and the second ending in **–er.** They both add an extra consonant. The **–lis** turns to **–llimus**, the **–er** adjectives to **–rrimus.**

Examples:

Positive	Comparative	Superlative
Facilis (easy)	facilior-ius (easier)	Facillimus-a-um (easiest)
Similis (like)	Similior-ius (more like)	Simillimus-a-um (most like)
Pulcher (beautiful)	Pulcherior-ius (more beautiful)	Pucherrimus-a-um)most beautiful)
Acer, acris, acre (keen, sharp)	Acrior, acrius(keener)	Acerrimus-a-um (keenest)

Other adjectives that follow this pattern: difficilis-e (difficult), gracilis (thin), humilis (low, humble), and liber(free).

Another group of irregular adjectives are so irregular that they all must be memorized. The redeeming grace of this whole chart is that memorizing them will be easy. First, because these adjectives are used so frequently, and secondly because the words are very similar to English ones.

Positive	Comparative	Superaltive
Bonus (good)	Melior-ius (better)	Optimus-a-um (best)
Magnus (great)	Maior-ius (greater)	Maximus (greatest)
Multus (much)	____,plus (more)	Plurimus-a-um (most)
Malus (bad)	Peior-ius (worse)	Pessimus-a-um (worst)
Parvus (little)	Minor, minus (smaller)	Minimus-a-um (smallest)
Superus-a-um (above)	Superior-ius (higher)	Summus-a-um (highest, furthest)
		Supremus-a-um (highest, last)

Practice: identify the degree of the adjective and then substitute the English with the Latin version.

Good

Higher

Little

Greatest

Better

Great

Smaller

Much

Best

most

Answers:

Positive, Bonus

Comparative, superior-ius

Positive, Parvus

Superlative, Maximus

Comparative, Melior, ius

Positive, Magnus

Comparative, minor

Positive, Multus

Superlative, Optimus

Superlative, Plurimus

Chapter 11
Verbs Principal Parts (Person, Number, Tense, Voice, Mood)

The verb is the powerhouse of the Latin sentence. The verb communicates a lot of information to a speaker or reader of the language. The reason for this is that verbs in Latin conjugate, meaning that they change their endings. These endings give a lot of clues about what is happening. There are five things that verbs can express.

Person:

Unlike English verbs in Latin express who is doing a sentence by the endings they have. First person means that the verb has an I or we subject. Second person means that subject of the verb has a you or you all subject. Third person means that the verb has a he/she/it or they subject.

Singular	**Plural**
I	We
You	You all
He, she, it	They

Number:

As you can see in the chart above Verbs can tell us number or whether the subjects of the sentence are singular or plural.

Tense: Verb tense tells us when something has happened. There are six verb tenses in Latin. Present tense, meaning the action of the verb is happening now. Imperfect tense, meaning the action is happening in the past but still ongoing. Perfect tense meaning the action has happened in the past. There is also pluperfect tense, future tense, and future perfect.

Voice: Refers to whether a verb is active or passive. Active voice is when the subject is doing the verb. Passive voice is when the subject of the sentence is being acted upon.

Mood: Three different moods in Latin refer to the indicative, Subjunctive and imperative. The indicative voice simply states facts or events as they are. Subjunctive voice communicates potential or theoretical action. The imperative voice communicates demands to an understood person.

There are four conjugations or groups of verbs in Latin. They all have their own patterns and characteristics. The first conjugation is one of the most simple and uniform of the bunch.

Chapter 11.1
First conjugation

Similar to the way that Latin nouns are listed with two forms in a typical Latin dictionary, most Latin verbs are listed with four forms. These are called the principal parts of the verb. The forms of the verb **laudo, laudare** is given as an example below.

Laudo-first person, singular, present, active, indicative

Laudare present active infinitive

Laudavi first person singular perfect active indicative

Laudatum perfect passive participle

This may seem overwhelming, but all first declension verbs (save a few exceptions) follow this exact same pattern. So, it is quite easy to remember them. To get started all you really need to know is the infinitive of the verb. It is from the infinitive of the verb that you find the stem.

The simplest way to remember how to find the stem of any verb is to find the infinitive. Depending on their conjugation infinitives will end with **-are**, **-ere**, **-ere**, **-ire**. The first conjugation infinitive sign is **-are**. For the first example I will use **Laudare** and take of the **–re** ending. So we have:

Lauda

It is to this stem that we add the present active indicative endings.

Present Tense

Singular	Plural
O	**Mus**
S	**Tis**
T	**Nt**

So them we have:

Laudo--> *I praise**

Laudas--> *You praise*
Laudat--> *he/she/it praises*
Laudamus--> *we praise*
Laudatis--> *You all praise*
Laudant--> *They praise.*

*note that in the first person the –a is dropped from the stem and it is simply **laudo**. That is consistent throughout all the verbs in the conjugation.

Practice: Find the stem of these verbs:

Spectare (to watch)

Amare(to love)

Ambulare (to walk)

Habitare (to dwell in, to live in)

Laborare (to work)

Practice two: translate these verbs:

Laboras

Ambulatis

Habitamus

Specto

Amat

Laborant

Ambulamus

Spectat

Answers

Specta

Ama

Ambula

Habita

labora

Practice two answers

You work

You all walk

We dwell in

I watch

He/she/it loves

They work

he/she/it watches

Second Conjugation

The second conjugation is much like the first conjugation with many verbs that follow the same pattern in their principal parts. A common verb that follows the typical pattern is **Habeo, Habere.** The second conjugation has more variation in patterns than the first but is still reasonably consistent.

Habeo- first person, singular, present, active, indicative

Habere-present active infinitive

Habui- First person, singular, perfect, active, indicative

Habitum-perfect passive participle

To find the stem we remove the **–re** from the infinitive and find the stem:

Habe

Then add the present active indicative endings:

Habeo-->*I have*
Habes-->*you have*
Habet-->*he/she/it have*
Habemus--> *we have*
Habetis--> *you all have*
Habent--> *they have*

Practice one: find the stem for these second conjugation verbs

Docere (to teach)
Abstinere (to refrain)
Audere (to dare)
Debere (to owe)
Tenere (to hold)
Delere (to destroy)

Practice two: Translate these verbs

Tenet
Doces
Audet
Deletis
Docent
Abstineo
Audemus
Delet
Docemus
Abstinent
Tenent

Answers

Practice one
Doce (to teach)
Abstine (to refrain)
Aude (to dare)
Debe (to owe)
Tene (to have)
Dele (to destroy)
Practice two
He/she/it has
You teach
He/she/it dares
You all destroy
they teach
I refrain
We dare
He/she/it destroy
We teach
They refrain
They have

Chapter 12
Accusative and Dative Case

Identifying both the accusative and dative cases is essential for reading in Latin. Learning about these cases also illustrates one of the most important differences between English and Latin word order. Namely, that in Latin word order is more flexible than in English.

Take the sentence below:

The girl gives food to the boby.

This makes good sense in English. The girl verbs the direct object to the indirect object. Clarity is very dependent on word order In English. If I move the words around the meaning becomes unclear or is lost all together.

So the pattern for the typical order for the English sentence is Subject+verb+object+indirect object.

Because the nouns in Latin have endings that determine their function in the sentence word order can be much more flexible. The Romans however did favor putting the main verb of their sentence at the end. They found this the most stylistically pleasing word order.

So, one often sees the patterns: Subject+object+verb or Subject+indirect object+ object +verb or direct object +indirect object+subject+verb.

The **accusative case** was the ending that signified the direct object of the verb, or the thing that is acted upon by the verb.

The **dative case** was the ending that signified the indirect object of the verb, or to whom or for whom the action was done.

The accusative case is bolded in the examples below:

Puella **cibum** dat. -->The girl gives food.

Canem puella dat. -->The girl gives a dog.

Puer **gladium** dat. --> The boy gives a sword.

Miles **futes** tenent. --> the soldiers hold clubs.

Magister **pueros et puellas** docet. --> The teacher teaches the boys and girls.

The dative case is bolded in the examples below:

Puella **puero** cibum dat. --> The Girl gives food to the boy.

Canem **pueris** magister dat. --> The teacher gave a dog to the boys.

Poeta **regi** carmen dat.--> The poet give a poem to the king.

Puellae **militibus** carmina cantat. --> The girls sing songs for the soldiers.

Practice: Identify the accusatives in these sentences

Puer puellae canem dat.

Mercator militibus gladium vendit.

Servi domino cibum dant,

Pueri et puellae magistri panem dant.

Mater rosas puellae dat.

Practice: Identify the datives in these sentences

Puer puellae canem dat.

Mercator militibus gladium vendit.

Servi domino cibum dant,

Pueri et puellae magistri panem dant.

Mater rosas puellae dat.

Practice two: Identify the correct translation for each sentence

Puer puellae canem dat.

a. The boy gives the girl to a dog.

b. The boy gives a dog to the girl.

Mercator militibus gladium vendit.

a. The Merchant sells a sword to the soldiers.

b. The Merchant sells soldiers to swords.

Servi domino cibum dant.

a. The servants give the master to the food.

b. The servants give food to the master.

Pueri et puellae magistri panem dant.

a. The boys and girls give bread to the teacher.

b. The boys give bread to the teacher and girls.

Mater rosas puellae dat.

a. The mother gives the girls to the roses.

b. The mother gives roses to the girls.

Answers:

Canem
Gladium
Cibum
Panem
Rosas
Puellae
Militibus

Domino

Magistri

Puellae

Exercise two

B

A

B

A

b

Chapter 13
The Third and Fourth Conjugation

The third conjugation is much more complex than the other three Latin conjugations. First, any student will notice that it has a similar infinitive ending to the second declension—**ere**. This may cause some confusion as to how to tell the difference. The answer to that question is that the second declension has a long **–e** often marked with a macron to show its length. The third conjugation has a short **–e**. This fact leads the third conjugation to have several irregularities in the present tense endings. They differences must be noted and simply memorized. Below is an example of a common third conjugation verb, **Duco, Ducere.**

Duco-first person, single, active, indicative

Ducere-present active infinitive

Duxi-First person, perfect, active, indicative

Ductum-present passive participle

To find the stem we drop the-**re** and get:

Duce

Remember that since that -**e** is short it turns into an **–i**

O	imus
is	itis
it	unt

So the full conjugation would really look like this.

Duco--> *I lead*
Ducis--> *you lead*
Ducit--> *he/she/ it leads*
Ducimus--> *We lead*
Ducitis--> *You all lead*
Ducunt--> *They lead*

The other thing that makes the third conjugation so difficult is that the principal parts are irregular and must be memorized in full. Here is a list of different verbs to give you an idea of the variety of third conjugation verbs.

Capio, capere, cepi, captum-to sieze*

Facio, facere, feci, factum –to do, make*

Fugio, fugere, fugi, fugitus-to flee*

Mitto, mittere, misi, missum-to send

Pono, ponere, posui, positum-to put, to place

Curro, currere, cucurri, cursus –to run

Traho, trahere, traxi, tractum-to drag

Duco, ducere, duxi, ductum-to lead

*these three nouns are part of a small group of verbs called third conjugation –**io** verbs. They conjugate in the same manner as fourth conjugation verbs.

Practice: fill in the missing principal part

Capio, capere, _____, captum

Facio, facere, feci, _____

Fugio, _____, fugi, fugitus

Mitto, mittere, _____, missum

_____, pontere, posui, positum

Curro, currere, _____, cursus

Traho, _____, traxi, tractum

_____, ducere, duxi, ductum

Answers:

Cepi
Factum
Fugere
Misi
Pono
Cucurri
Trahere
Duco

The Fourth Conjugation

The fourth conjugation is similar to the first in that it has very regular principal parts. The infinitive ending that characterizes this conjugation is – ire.

Dormio- first person, singular, present, active, indicative

Dormire-present active infinitive

Dormivi-first person, singular, perfect, active indicative

Dormitum-perfect passive participle

To find the stem remove the **–re** from the infinitive.

Dormi

Then add the present active endings to conjugate.

Dormio-*I sleep*
Dormis-*you sleep*
Dormit-*he/she/it sleeps*
Dormimus-*we sleep*
Dormitis-*you all sleep*
Dormiunt-*they sleep*

Practice: Find the stem of these fourth conjugation verbs.

Dormire (to sleep)
Audire (to hear)
Scire (to know)
Venire (to come)
Sentire (to sense, feel)

Practice two: translate the following verbs

Dormimus
Venio

Scis
Audit
Dormiunt
Venimus
Scitis
Veniunt
Sentis
audimus

Answers:

Dormi
Audi
Sci
Veni
Senti

Practice two answers

We sleep
I come
You know
She/he/it hears
They sleep
We come
You all know
They come
You feel
We hear

We come to our review of the last two Latin cases: the genitive and ablative. The genitive case is fairly straight forward in usage in comparison to the ablative case. The ablative case can be tricky to master with many different uses and rules governing it.

There are three main uses of the **genitive case** to show possession, description, and parts of a whole. The genitive case is typically translated with the preposition **of**.

The genitive is used to convey the idea of possession as in the examples below.

Panis Matris--> The bread of Mother or Mother's bread.

Milites regis--> The soldier of the king or the King's Soldiers.

Gladius domini--> The sword of the master or the Master's sword.

Magister puellarum--> The teacher of the girls or the girls' teacher

Canis puerorum --> The dog of the boys or the boys' dog.

The genitive is also used to describe a person or thing if used with an adjective.

Vir magnae virtutis--> a man of great strength

Puella formae sanae--> a girl of healthy shape

Mater magni armoris--> a mother of great love

Canis magnae celeritas--> a dog of great speed

The genitive is also used to represent the part of a whole. This usage is also called the partitive genitive.

Satis panis--> enough of bread

Plus aquae--> more of water

Pars legionis--> part of the legion

Nihil amoris--> nothing of love

The **Ablative case** is often called the adverbial case because it often describes how the verb is done. I'll list several ablative usages (but not all) in order to give a feel for how the case works.

The ablative of means tells the reader by what means the action of the verb was done.

Lunam oculis meis video--> I see the moon with my eyes (by means of my eyes).

Petram equo trahit--> He dragged the rock with a horse (by means of a horse.)

The ablative of manner tells in what manner or how the verb was done. The ablative of manner is use with and without the preposition cum.

Milites magna cum audacia ducet.--> He lead the soldiers with great boldness.

Magna cum cura dico.--> I speak with great care.

The ablative of accompaniment tells us with whom the verb is done. This construction is always used with the preposition cum.

Bellum cum Caesare gessit.--> he waged war with Caesar.

Cum domino venit.--> he came with the master.

 The ablative of time give the reader the clue of when an event occurred. This construction is always used with out any prepositions and always has some unit of time involved and so it easy to recognize.

Una hora magister venit.--> The teacher came at the first hour.

Mense martio exit.--> He leaves in the month of march.

Practice one: State which genitive appears below. Then translate.

Mater magnae sapientiae
Canis magistri
Pars horti
Puer magnae virtutis
Nihil aquae
Cubiculum Caesaris

Practice two: identify the ablative phrases below. Then Translate

hora secunda dormimus.
Cum matre Canto.
Magna cum celeritate currit.
Milites gladio interfecunt.
Cum nauta venit.
Magna cum lauda venit.
Hora tertia venit.
In urbam equo venit. (urbam-city)

Practice one answers:

Description. Mother of great wisdom.
Possessive. Dog of the master.
Genitive of the whole or partitive. Part of the garden
Description. Boy of great strength.
Genitive of the whole or partitive. Nothing of water
Possessive. Bedroom of Caesar.

Practice two answers:

Ablative of time. We sleep at the second hour.
Ablative of accompaniment. I sing with mother.
Ablative of manner. He runs with great swiftness.
Ablative of means. The soldiers kill with a sword.
Ablative of accompaniment. He comes with a sailor.
Ablative of manner. He comes with great praise.

Ablative of time. He comes at the third hour.
Ablative of means. He comes into the city by means of a horse.

Chapter 15
Future, Imperfect, and Perfect Verb Tenses

We have only worked with sentences that were in present tense. Latin has six verb tenses present, imperfect, perfect, pluperfect, future and future perfect. In this chapter I will explain the future, imperfect and perfect verb tenses.

Forming the future tense is slightly complicated by the fact that the first and second conjugation are done differently than the third and fourth. The first and second conjugations are very straight forward. Just find the stem of the verb, as we did with present tense, and add the future active indicative endings as shown below.

Singular	Plural
Bo	Bimus
Bis	Bitis
Bit	Bunt

The third and fourth conjugations add the below endings to their stems. The third conjugation is unusual because it lengthens the short –i characteristic of its stem to an **e**. While the fourth conjugations keep its long –i stem and add an -**e**

Am	Emus
Es	Etis
Et	Ent

Chart of future active indicative conjugations in verbs 1-4

Laudabo	Tenebo	Ducam	Dormiam
Laudabis	Tenebis	Duces	Dormies
Laudabit	Tenebit	Ducet	Dormiet
Laudabimus	Tenebimus	Ducemus	Dormiemus
Laudabitis	Tenebitis	Ducetis	Dormietis
Laudabunt	Tenebunt	Ducent	Dormient

Practice: Translate these verbs

Laudabitis

Tenebis
Duces
Dormiam
Tenebit
Ducent
Laudabunt
Dormiemus

Answers:

You all will praise
You will have
You lead
I will sleep
He will have
They will lead
They will praise
We will sleep.

The imperfect tense

The imperfect tense doesn't have a perfect match up in English. The verb is a past action that was still continuing, but not finished. So, its translation into English can be flexible depending on the context. Most books recommend translating with a to be and –ing verb.

Examples:

Laudabam-->I was praising
Laudabas--> You were praising
Laudabat--> he/she/it were praising
Laudabamus-->we were praising
Laudabatis--> You all were praising
Laudabant --> They were praising

The imperfect is formed by adding these endings to the regular verb stems. Notice that fourth conjugation adds an **–e** to its stem.

Singular	Plural
Bam	**Bamus**

Bas   **Batis**

Bat   **Bant**

Chart of imperfect active indicative conjugations 1-4

Laudabam	Tenebam	Ducebam	Dormiebam
Laudabas	Tenebas	Ducebas	Dormiebas
Laudabat	Tenebat	Ducebat	Dormiebat
Laudabamus	Tenebamus	Ducebamus	Dormiebamus
Laudabatis	Tenebatis	Ducebatis	Dormiebatis
Labudabant	tenebant	Ducebant	Dormiebant

Practice: Translate these verbs

Laborabamus
Veniebam
Tenebas
Ponebant
Dormiebatis
veniebat
ponebamus
laborabas

Answers:

We were working
I was coming
You were having
They were placing
You all were sleeping
He was coming
We were placing
You were working.

Future and Imperfect of verb sum, esse

While we are doing imperfect and future verb tense it is also convenient to show the paradigms for the to be verb-sum, esse. These form are irregular and must be memorized.

Future of sum, esse

Ero	Erimus
Eris	Eritis
Erit	Erunt

Imperfect of sum, esse

Eram	Eramus
Eras	Earatis
Erat	Errant

The Perfect Tense

The perfect tense is quite easy to form, especially now that you are familiar with how to conjugate verbs in Latin. I have spoken before of principal parts. The second of these being the infinitive and explaining how it was the key to finding the present stem. Now that we are in the perfect (past) tense we must use the perfect active stem. The perfect active stem is found in the third principal part. Then all that remains is to add the perfect active endings below.

Perfect active indicative endings

Singular	Plural
I	Imus
Isti	Istis
It	Erunt

Chart of Perfect active indicative conjugations 1-4

Laudavi	Tenui	Duxi	Dormivi
Laudavisti	Tenuisti	Duxisti	Dormivisti
Laudavit	Tenuit	Duxit	Dormivit
Laudavimus	Tenuimus	Duximus	Dormivimus
Laudavistis	Tenuistis	Duxistis	Dormivitis
Laudaverunt	tenuerunt	duxerunt	dormiverunt

The best way to translate the perfect to English is as a simple past tense verb.

Example:

Laudavi--> I praised
Laudavisti--> you praised
Laudavit--> he/she/it praised
Laudavimus--> We praised
Laudavistis--> you all praised
Laudaverunt--> They praised

Practice: Translate these verbs

Duxi
Dormivisti
Tenuerunt
Laboravit
Tenuistis
Duximus
Duxit
Dormivi
Answers
I led
You slept
They held
He/she/it worked
You all held
We led
He/she/it led
I slept

Extended practice:

Identify the verb tense and then translate

Actores in theatro spectavimus.

Septa hora in horto ambulabas.

Puella cibum in cubiculum tenebit.

Rex milites in urbem misit.

poetas magnae artis audiam.

 In horto laborabatis.

Magister libro pueros et puellas docuit.

Fortuna bellum spectare audebit.

Canes in urbe cucurrerunt.

Hodie milities et nautae venient.

In cubiculum matris dormiebas.

Answers:

Perfect. We watched the actors in the theater.

Imperfect. You were walking in the garden at the seven hour.

 Future. The girl will have food in the bedroom.

Perfect. The king sent soldiers into the city.

Future. I will hear poets of great skill.

Imperfect. You all were working in the garden.

Perfect. The teacher was teaching the boys and girls by means of a book.

Future. Fortuna will dare to watch war.

Perfect. The dogs ran in the city.

Future. Today the soldiers and sailors will come.

Imperfect. You were sleeping in mother's bedroom.

Perfect Infinitive

We have already become familiar with the present active infinitive. There are six infinitives in Latin. Now that you know the perfect stem you can also form the perfect active infinitive. To form the perfect active infinitive simply take the perfect stem and add **–isse.**

Laudavisse   Tenuisse   Duxisse   Dormivisse

Laudavisse-->to have praised
Tenuisse--> to have held
Duxisse-->to have led
Dormivisse-->to have slept

Practice: Identify these infinitives as present or perfect active and then translate.

Spectare
Laudavisse
Dormire
Venire
Duxisse
Mittere
Venisse
Docuisse
ducere
specatvisse

Answers:

present, to watch
perfect, to have praised
present, to sleep
present, to come
perfect, to have led
present, to send
perfect, to have come
perfect. To have taught
present, to lead
perfect, to have watched

We have spent a lot of time talking about infinitives and how they help us find the present stem in order to conjugate verbs, but it is important to know that the infinitive has other uses. I will go over two common uses for the infinitive: the complementary infinitive and indirect statement.

The complementary infinitive

The complementary infinitive is used when a verb needs a helper infinitive to complete its meaning. We see this often in English. I wish to do_____. I need to do_____. I am able to do_____. The words "to do" are key clues that you are using an infinitive.

Several Latin verbs that take a complementary infinitive are volo, nolo, possum, debeo.

Example:

Dormire volo.--> I wish to sleep.
Audire debes.--> you ought to listen.
Currere potest.--> he can run or he is able to run.

Irregular verb volo, velle-to wish

Volo	**Volumus**
Vis	**Vultis**
Vult	**Volunt**

Irregular verb nolo, nolle-not to wish

Nolo	**Nolumus**
Non vis	**Non vultis**
Non vult	**Nolunt**

Practice: Translate

Nolo hodie currere.

Vis carmina in theatro cantare.

Volumus et puellas et pueros docere.

Non vis in villa hodie laborare.

Volumus puellas audire.

Non vultis actores in theatro spectare.

Volunt pecuniam in therma invenire. (pecunia-money)

Answers:

I don't wish to run today.

You wish sing songs in the theater.

We wish to teach both girls and boys.

We do not wish to work in the house today.

We wish to hear the girls.

You all do not wish to watch the actors in the theater.

They wish to find money in the baths

Indirect statement

An indirect statement is a sentence that reports what someone else has said. An indirect statement is not a direct quote but a report of what someone else was thinking and saying.

Latin does do direct quotation in a similar way to English. So do not be confused and think that an indirect statement is really a direct quote. To show how the two contrast I give an example of a direct statement below.

Mater inquit, "hodie pater veniebit." --> Mother said, "Father comes today."

However, sometimes the need to explain what someone says indirectly arises. In English it looks like this:

Mom says that dad is coming today.

To convey the same idea in Latin we use an indirect statement.

Mater dicit hodie patrem venire.

An indirect statement is broken down into these parts:

An introductory verb of feeling, knowing, or saying.

The subject of the statement in the accusative case.

An infinitive.

A funny popular example of indirect statement can be found in the Coldplay music video "Christmas Lights." The words, "**Credo Elvem etiam viver**e" light up on the top of the stage. I believe that Elvis still lives is the translation.

Practice: Translate

Credimus ad villam patrem venire.

Scio canes per via currere.

Scis prima hora puellas ambulare.

Credunt nautas navi cibum mittere. (navis-is ship)

Audio dominum in villam pueros mittere.

Livia audit milites nunc venire.

Scio milites cibum et aquam capere.

Credo Matrem cibum invenire.

Answers:

We believe father is coming to the house.

I know that the dogs were running through the street.

You know that the girls walk at the first hour.

They believe that the sailors are sending food to the ship.

I heard that the master send the boys into the house.

Livia heard that the soldiers are coming now.

I know that the soliders are taking food and water.

I believe that mother is finding food.

Imperatives

So far we have learned about the indicative mood. One of the three verb moods in Latin: indicative, imperative, and subjunctive. The imperative mood conveys a sense of commanding or ordering the person who is spoken to. It is quite simple to form.

The singular imperative is the same as the present active stem.

Lauda me!--> praise me!
Specta me!--> look at me!

Singular:

Lauda (praise)   Doce (teach)   Duce (lead)   Dormi (sleep)

To form the plural imperative all one needs to do is add **–te** to the stem.

Plural:
Laudate   Docete   Ducite   Dormite

To form the negative imperative one must use a different construction. Using the imperatives of the verb nolo and an infinitive was used to express a negative command.

Noli dicere!--> don't speak!
Nolite laborare!--> don't work!

Practice: Translate

Amate me!
Nolite ambulare! Currete!
Habita cum me!
Noli spectare!
Aude!
Nolite abstinere.
Delete
Carpe diem
Audite

Answers

(you all) love me!
(you all) Do not walk! Run!
Live with me!
Don't look at me
Dare!
(you all) don't refrain.
(you all) destroy
Seize the day
(you all) listen

Chapter 17
The Subjunctive Mood

The last and third verb mood in Latin is the subjunctive. The subjunctive mood is the opposite of the indicative. While the indicative mood reports facts and happenings as they occur. The subjunctive is the mood of possibility, theory, and potential. There is an extensive list of phrases wherein it is grammatically correct to use the subjunctive in speaking and writing. I will list a few common ones here, but will hardly attempt a comprehensive list in a book that serves as an introduction to Latin grammar.

First we must go over how to form a subjunctive verb in the present indicative active. In previous chapters we mentioned how each verb had a perfect active stem and these stems had vowels that were indicative of a verb's conjugation. The vowels change to indicate their subjunctive status. Use the mnemonic: we fear a liar.

First conjugation **a** stem changes to **e**.

Second conjugation long **e** stem changes to **ea**.

Third conjugation short **e** turns to **a**.

Fourth conjugation **i** turns into a **ia**.

Laudem	Teneam	Ducam	Dormiam
Laudes	Teneas	Ducas	Dormias
Laudet	Teneat	Ducat	Dormiat
Laudemus	Teneamus	Ducamus	Dormiamus
Laudetis	Teneatis	Ducatis	Dormiatis
Laudent	Teneant	Ducant	Dormiant

The imperfect tense of the subjunctive is extremely easy to form and to recognize. Simply take the infinitive and add the present tense personal endings. Note that the first person ending turns to an **–m**.

Laudarem	Tenerem	Ducerem	Dormirem
Laudares	Teneres	Duceres	Dormires
Laudaret	Teneret	Duceret	Dormiret
Laudaremus	Teneremus	Duceremus	Dormiremus

| Laudaretis | Teneretis | Duceretis | Dormiretis |
| Laudarent | tenerent | Ducerent | Dormirent |

The subjunctive verb governs a decent number of specific phrases types. How the subjunctive verb is translated often relies on the context of the phrase it is found in. Most subjunctive verbs are part of subordinate clauses, but there are a few of them that govern independent clauses. That brings us to our first use of the subjunctive.

The jussive clause is a clause that communicates a command or order of what you should do. So it is often translated with a should/ought/let construction. A negative command is introduce with **–ne.**

Examples:

Rex nunc Inveniat.--> let the king come now, the king should come now.

Pueri dormiant.--> Let the boys sleep, the boys should sleep.

Puella matrem et paterm laudet.--> Let the girl praise mother and father, the girls should praise mother and father.

An Indirect question in Latin always has a subjunctive verb. Similar to an indirect statement an indirect question is one that is not asked directly. An indirect question is easy to identify from other subjunctive types because it is always introduced with a question word **like quis/quid, qui, quae, quo, ubi, quot, quantus, num or quomodo.**

Centurio rogavit quis verba regis audivisset. -->The centurion asked who had heard the words of the king.

Senauts congnoverunt ubi captivus esset.--> The senate knew where the captive was.

The purpose clause is a subordinate clause that gives the purpose or reason for the action in the previous part of the sentence. We often use an infinitive in English to express purpose, but Latin more often uses the subjunctive purpose clause. So it feels natural to translate the purpose clause as an infinitive. Other phrases that are commonly used are: so that

and in order that. Purpose clauses are introduced with the conjunction **ut**. If the purpose clause is negative it is introduced with a **ne**.
Examples:

Milites venerunt ut verbum regis audiret. -->the soldiers came so that they might hear the words of the king.

Discipuli audiunt ut docent.--> Students listen so they may learn.

Nauta currit ne dominum audiat.--> The sailor runs in order not to listen to the master.

The result clause is very similar to the purpose clause. Except, as it is named, serves to convey the result of the action taken in previous clause. The result clause is also introduced by the conjunction **ut**, but often also has an adverb like **tam**, **ita**, or **sic**.

Tam magnus erat rex ut populi eum amarent.--> so great was the king that the people loved him.
Mater tot pueros misit ut in una die villam faceret.--> The mother sent so many boys that they made the house in one day.

Practice: Identify the subjunctive clause and then translate it.

Pater rogavit quis puerum interfecisset.

Amici ad urbem currit ut equos et aurigas (charioteer) spectent.

Fortitudio (courage) puerorum laudet.

Veni ut loquerer tecum.

Tanta erat fortitude militum ut perire potius quam fugere vellent. (potius quam=rather than)

Ad urbem hodie ambulemus.

Me rogaverunt num satis aquae haberet. (num-whether)

Venisti ut cursum(race) spectares.

Tot canes in via ambulant ut eos militibus daremus.

Nuntios nesciebat cur milites navem aedificarent. (nescieabat-to not know, aedificarent-to build)

Tam diligenter cenam paravi ut dominus me laudaret. (paravi-to prepare)

Puella ad theatrum venit ut saltare discat. (saltare-dance, Discat-to learn)

Tot verba dixit ut populi dormirent.

Cognoscere volumus cur consul senators exire iuberet. (iuberet-ordered, exire-to leave)

Mater equum cepit ut paterm inveniret.

Answers:

Indirect question. The father asked who killed the boy.

Purpose clause. The friends ran to the city to look at the horses and charioteers. Or the friends ran to the city in order to look at the horses and charioteers.

Jussive clause. Let us praise the strength of the boys.

Purpose clause. I came so that I might speak with you.

Result clause. So great was the courage of the soldiers that they wished to die rather than to flee.

Jussive clause. Let us walk to the city today.

Indirect question. They asked me whether I had enough of water.

Purpose clause. You came so that you might watch the race.

Result clause. I prepared the meal so diligently that the master praised me.

Result clause. So many dogs were walking in the streets that we gave them to the soldiers.

Indirect question. The messengers did not know why the soldiers were building the boat.

Purpose clause. The girl came to the theater to learn to dance.

Result clause. He spoke so many words that the people were sleeping.

Indirect question. We wish to know why the consul ordered the senators to leave.

Purpose clause. Mother took a horse so that she might find father.

Chapter 18
Datives Continued

In previous chapters we covered the dative case. In that section we only talked about how datives were used as indirect objects. While this is an important use of the dative case there are several others that it would be good to introduce. There are three types of verbs that treat dative case differently: special verbs, compound verbs, and impersonal verbs.

Datives with Special verbs

There are some verbs in Latin that are intransitive. An intransitive verb is one that cannot take a proper object. So these verbs cannot take an accusative case and instead they take the dative case. Often they are translated into English as if they were transitive with the help of the preposition to. These verbs often have meanings that require the verb to do something to a person like help, threaten, pardon, spare, trust, harm, envy, favor, command, obey, serve etc.

These special verbs are quite numerous and it isn't really practical to memorize each one, but simply knowing some common verbs that take this construct can help in reading and translating Latin. Then if you run into an odd sentence that seems to follow this pattern it will be easy to look up the verb in the dictionary and see if it takes the dative case.

Parco, parcere—to spare
Placeo, placere(2)—to be pleasing to
Servio, servire—to serve, be a slave to
Studeo, studere(2)—to be zealous toward, to study
Credo, credere- to believe, to trust
Noceo, Nocere (2)- to do harm to

Examples:

Placeo patri--> I please my father
Servis domino--> You serve the master
Credebam tibi-->I was trusting you
Studeo linguae latinae-->I study the Latin tongue
Nocet nautae--> I do harm to the sailor

Dative with compound verbs

Compound verbs often take the dative case, especially when the compound verb has a meaning very different from the original verb.

Example:

Video nauta--> I see the sailor
Invideo nautae.--> I envy the sailor.

Compound verbs can also be translated as the object of the preposition attached to the front of the verb and in some cases the verb may have an accusative object as well.

Example:

Praeposui poetam servis.--> I put the poet in charge of the slaves.
Puellis Praestant--> they stand before the girls.

Practice: translate

Mater mihi non credit.
Parce servo.
Studeo mathematicae.
Magister pueros puellis praesposuit.
Poeta magistro invidet.

Answers:

Mother does not believe me.
Spare the slave.
I study math.
The teacher placed the boys before the girls.
The poet envies the teacher.

Chapter 19
Passive Voice

We have covered most of the different aspects of Latin verbs, learning the indicative, imperative and subjunctive moods. Now, we come to the aspect of tense. Previously, we have only learned about active verbs. This chapter introduces the passive voice endings for the present, imperfect, future, and perfect tenses. The active voice is called so because the nominative subject is the done doing the action of the verb. The subject is a mover, shaker and go getter. In the passive voice the nominative takes the back seat and is a passive agent in the sentence.

Active: The teacher taught the children.

Passive: The children were taught by the teacher.

In English we favor the active voice and feel that the passive voice is undesirable unless your communications necessitates an avoidance of responsibility. So, that is why the passive voice can sometimes be difficult to translate because we are told to avoid using it, and thus have less practice. The Romans, however, had less of a problem with using the passive voice and use it quite a bit more frequently than we would see in English. So, it is a good idea to get started with practicing.

Present Passive endings

R	Mur
Ris	Mini
Tur	Ntur

Examples of Present passive conjugations 1-4

Laudor	Doceor	Ducor	Audior
Laudaris	Doceris	Duceris*	Audiris
Laudatur	Docetur	Ducitur	Auditor
Laudamur	Docemur	Ducimur	Audimur
Laudamini	Docemini	Ducimini	Audimini
Laudantur	Docentur	Ducuntur	Audiuntur

*note that the second person passive of the third declension and **-io** verbs are irregular and turns into

-eris.

The passive form of these verbs are usually translated into English with the to be verb. The subject is "being" rather than doing. The chart below show all the translations for the verbs above.

I am praised or I am being praised.	I am taught or I am being taught.	I am led or I am being led.	I am heard or I am being heard.
You are praised	You are taught	You are led	You are heard
He/she/ it is praised	He/she/it is taught	He/she/it is led	He/she/it is heard
We are praised	We are taught	We are led	We are heard
You all are	You all are taught	You all are led	You all are heard
They are praised	They are taught	They are led	They are heard

Practice: Translate these verbs into English

Laudaris
Ducor
Audimini
Docentur
Laudor
Docetur
Ducuntur
Laudamur
Audior
Ducimur
audiris

Answers:

You all are praised or you all are being praised
I am led or I am being led
You all are heard or you all are being heard
They are taught or they are being taught
I am praised or I am being praised
He/she/it are taught or he/she/it are being taught
They are led or they are being led
We are praised or we are being praised

I am heard or I am being heard
We are led or we are being led
You are heard or you are being heard.

The passive infinitive

Now that we have learned the passive tense I'll introduce the passive infinitive. The infinitive endings are added to the same stem as always. The first conjugation changes from **-are** to **-ari**, the second from **-ere** to **-eri**, the third for **-ere** to **-i**, the fourth **-ire** to **-iri**.

Laudari   Doceri   duci   Audiri

laudari--> to be praised
doceri--> to be taught
duci--> to be led
audiri--> to be heard

Practice: identify the infinitive as active or passive then translate

docere
spectari
faci
habere
veniri
laudare
spectare
dormiri
curri

Answers:

active, to teach
passive, to be watched
passive, to do
active, to have
passive, to be coming
active, to praise
active, to watch
passive, to sleep

passive, to run

Imperfect Passive verbs

In previous sections were learned about the imperfect tense. The imperfect tense is a past tense that conveys ongoing or continuous action. It is formed by taking the present active stem adding **–ba**, and then adding the passive endings. See all the forms of conjugations 1-4 in the chart below.

Laudabar	Docebar	Ducebar	Audiebar
Laudabaris	Docebaris	Ducebaris	Audiebaris
Laudabatur	Docebatur	Ducebatur	Audiebatur
Laudabamur	Docebamur	Ducebamur	Audiebamur
Laudabamini	Docebamini	Ducebamini	Audiebamini
Laudabantur	Docebantur	Ducebantur	Audiebantur

I was being praised	I was being taught	I was being led	I was being heard
You were being praised	You were being taught	You were being led	You were being heard
He/she/it was being praised	He/she/it was being taught	He/she/it was being led	He/she/it was being heard
We were being praised	We were being taught	We were being led	We were being heard
You all were being praised	You all were being taught	You all were being led	You all were being heard
They were being praised	They were being taught	They were being led	They were being heard

Practice: Translate these verbs into English

Laudabantur
Ducebar
Docebaris
Audiebamini
Docebamur
Laudabaris
Ducebatur
Audiebantur
Laudabatur

Docebamini

Answers:

They were being praised
I was being led
You were being taught
You all were being heard
We were being taught
You were being praised
He/she/it was led
They were being heard
He/she/it was praised.

Future passive

The future passive is similar to how the future in the active tense is formed. The first and second conjugations rely on adding the **–bi** plus the passive endings. The third and fourth conjugations both change the vowel in their stems to become longer. Therefore, the short **–e** turns to a long **–e** in third declension. The fourth conjugation adds an **–e** also. Notice that **–bi** changes to **–be** in the second person singular and to **-bu** in the third person plural.

Laudabor	Docebor	Ducar	Audiar
Laudaberis	Doceberis	Duceris	Audieris
Laudabitur	Docebitur	Ducetur	Audietur
Laudabimur	Docebimur	Ducemur	Audiemur
Laudabimini	Docebimini	Ducemini	Audiemini
Laudabuntur	Docebuntur	ducentur	Audientur

I shall/will be praised	I shall/will be taught	I shall/will be led	I shall/will be heard
You shall/will be praised	you shall/will be taught	You shall/will be led	You shall/will be heard
He/she/it shall/will be praised.	He/she/it shall/will be taught.	He/she/it shall/will be led	He/she/it shall/will be heard
We shall/will be praised.	We shall/will be taught	We shall/will be led	We shall/will be heard
You all shall/will	You all shall/will	You all shall/will	You all shall/will

be praised.	be taught	be led	be heard
They shall/will be praised.	They shall/will be taught	They shall/will be led	They shall/will be heard

Practice: translate the following verbs into English

laudabuntur
audiemur
ducar
Docebimini
Audietur
Laudabitur
Audieris

Answers:

They will/shall be praised
We will/shall be heard
I will/shall be led
You all will/shall be taught
He/she/it will/shall be heard
He/she/it will/shall be praised
You will/shall be heard

The perfect passive

Having reached the perfect passive indicative tense we have finally come to the point where I can explain how to use the fourth principal part. To form the perfect passive one must take the fourth principal part and add the correct conjugation of sum.

For a quick review we will review the four principal parts of our model verbs and then identify the fourth principal part.

Laudo, laudare, laudavi, ladatus
Doceo, docere, docui, doctus
Duco, ducere, duxi, ductus
Audio, audire, audivi, auditus

The fourth principal parts of these four verbs are: **laudatus, doctus, ductus, auditus**.

Something else that you need to know about the fourth principal part is that it is a participle--the perfect passive participle to be exact. A participle is a verb that has some noun qualities to it. Each participle you will notice ends with the familiar **–us** ending. That is because the forth principal part changes its endings just like a first and second declension adjective. The participle ending changes to match the nominative in the sentence.

Examples:

Puella laudata est. The girl has been praised.

Discipuli docti sunt. The students have been taught.

Milites ducti sunt. The soldiers have been led.

Carmina audita sunt. The songs have been heard.

To form the perfect passive verb simply use the fourth principal part and add the present form of **sum, esse**.

Laudatus-a-um sum	Doctus-a-um sum	Ductus-a-um sum	Auditus-a-um sum
Laudatus –a-um es	Doctus-a-um es	Ductus-a-um es	Auditus-a-um es
Laudatus-a-um est	Doctus-a-um est	Ductus-a-um est	Auditus-a-um est
Laudati-ae-a sumus	Docti-ae-a sumus	Ducti-ae-a sumus	Auditi-ae-a sumus
Laudati-ae-a estis	Docti-ae-a estis	Ducti-ae-a estis	Auditi-ae-a estis
Laudati-a-a sunt	Docti-ae-a sunt	Ducti-ae-a sunt	Auditi-ae-a sunt

The English translations for the perfect passive verb conjugations 1-4.

I have been praised or I was praised	I was taught or I have been taught	I was led or I have been led	I was heard or I have been heard
You have been	You were taught	You were led or	You were heard

praise or You were praised	or you have been taught	you have been led	or you have been heard
He/she/it was praised or he/she/it have been praised	He/she/it was taught or he/she/ it have been taught	He/she/it was taught or he/she/it have been taught	He/she/it were heard or he/she/it have been heard
We were praised or we have been praised	We were taught or we have been taught	We were led or we have been led	We were heard or we have been heard
You all were praised or you all have been praised	You all were taught or you all have been taught	You all were led or you all have been led	You all were heard or you all have been heard
They were praised or They have been praised	They were taught or they have been praised	They were led or you all have been led	They were heard or they have been heard

Practice: Translate

Doctus-a-um sum

Laudati-a-a sunt

Auditus-a-um es

Ducti-ae-a sumus

Auditi-ae-a estis

Ducti-ae-a sunt

Laudatus-a-um sum

Docti-ae-a sumus

Answers:

I was taught or I have been taught

They were praised or They have been praised

You were heard or you have been heard

We were led or we have been led

You all were heard or you all have been heard

They were led or they have been led

I was praised or I have been praised

We are taught or we have been taught.

The perfect passive infinitive

Now that we have learned the perfect passive tense, I'll introduce the perfect passive infinitive. The infinitive is formed by taking the perfect stem and adding **-esse.**

| Laudatus-a-um esse | Doctus-a-um esse | Ductus-a-um esse | Auditus-a-um esse |

Laudatus –a-um esse--> to have been praised
Doctus-a-um esse--> to have been taught
Ductus-a-um esse--> to have been led
Auditus-a-um esse--> to have been heard

Practice: Identify the infinitive as present passive or perfect passive then translate

Laudatus esse
Laudari
Audiri
Auditus esse
Dormivi
Duci
Spectatus esse
Ductus esse

Answers:

Perfect passive, to have been praised

Present passive, to be praised

Present passive, to be heard

Perfect passive, to have been heard

Present passive, to have slept

Present passive, to be led

Perfect passive, to have seen

Perfect passive, to have been led

Deponent verbs:

There are some verbs in Latin called deponent verbs. These verbs are a group of irregular verbs that have passive forms but active meanings. Several of these verbs are quiet common and it is useful to memorize them because of how often they are used and because they are irregular. If you run across a deponent verb in a Latin dictionary the principal parts will be in passive tense. This is the major clue to finding out if a verb is deponent.

Examples:

Hortor, hortari, hortatus- to urge, encourage

Fateor, fateri, fassus-to confess

Sequor, sequi, secutus- to follow

Molior, moliri, molitus-to work at

Patior, pati, passus-to suffer, endure

Arbitror, arbitrari, arbitratus- to judge, to think

Conor, conari, conatus-to try, attempt

Loquor, loqui, locutus-to say, speak

Nascor, nasci, natus sum-to be born

Morior, mori, mortuus-to die

SECTION 3:
LATIN CULTURE

Chapter 20
Roman Names

In ancient Rome each child was given a bulla by his or her parents, nine days (eight days for girls) after birth. The child also received his or her name on this day. A bulla was similar to a locket, which was worn around the neck with an amulet placed inside it to ward off evil. Rich families made bulla out of gold or silver, and poorer families often out of leather. Girls wore their bulla until they married, and then it was kept with other childhood toys or mementos. Boys wore their bulla until they reached manhood and obtained their *toga virilis.* A boy's bulla would be kept carefully in case they achieved a triumph. On that day they would wear the bulla to ward off the envy of other men.

The Roman Name

The Praenomen:

A *praenomen* is similar to our first given names today, but the options for this name were limited. That list included: Aulus (A), Decimus(D), Gaius(c), Gnaeus(Gn), Kaeso (k),m Lucius (L), Manius (M'), Marcus (M), Publius (P), Quintus (Q), Servius (Ser), Sextus (S), Spurius(S), Tiberius (TI), Titus (T)

The Nomen:

This name is similar to our surnames today, and identified the clan (gens) to which the person belonged. This name was passed from father to son with each generation.

The Cognomen:

A *cognomen* identified the branch of the clan to which the person belonged. This name was also passed to from father to son with each generation. The origins of these names are believed originally to be nicknames.

Examples: *Gaius Julius Caesar*

   Marcus Tullius Cicero

Note: Girls were given the feminine form of their father's *nomen*. If there was more than one daughter they were identified with *maior* and *minor*, or *prima*, *secunda*, *tertia*. Then the cognomen was added.
Example:

Julia Caesaris Maior
Tullia Ciceronis Prima

Chapter 21
Roman Family and Home

The Roman family was headed by the father or the Romans called him the *paterfamilias.* He was in charge of everyone in the family for as long as he was alive. Children were very important to Romans so they could pass on the family name. If a *paterfamilias* did not have a son to inherit then he would adopt—most likely a close relative. Girls were married in their mid-teens and were encouraged to run their households, managing the slaves, children, and important guests and visitors.

Rooms of a Roman house

Atrium	Atrium-the atrium of the roman house was very important, as it was the center of everything. It also had a pool called an impluvium that collected rainwater for the family to drink. It often held a shrine to honor ancestral gods.
Triclinium	This is the place where the family dined. The triclinium was often decorated with beautiful art and mosaics on the floor. The family ate lying down on couches. Many houses would have an indoor and outdoor dining room.
Tablinum	The study of the paterfamilias. Where he would meet important people.
Peristylium	A peristyle. The peristylum had the family garden in the center of it. Open to the sky, the rain was able to fall directly into the garden. Around the area of the garden was a covered porch surrounded by columns which held up the roof. This porch served as an entrance to all the cubiculi.
Cubiculum	Bedroom
Culina	Kitchen

Habetne villa culinam?—does the house have a kitchen?

Habetne villa triclinium?-does the house have a dining room?

Quot triclinium in villa habes? How many dining rooms does the house have?

Quot cubicula in villa habes? How many bedrooms does the house have?

The Roman Family

Pater	Father
Mater	Mother
Filius	Son
Filia	Daughter
Frater	Brother
Soror	Sister
Avia	Grandmother
Avus	Grandfather
Aunt (maternal)	Matertera
Aunt (paternal)	Amita
Uncle (maternal)	Avunculus
Uncle (paternal)	Patruus
Consobrinus	Cousin
Uxor	Wife
Maritus	Husband
Liberi	Children

Habisne liberos?--> do you have children?

Quot liberos habes?--> how many children do you have?

Habisne fratres et sorores?-->do you have brothers and sisters?

Quot fratres et sorores habes?—how many brothers and sisters do you have

Esne tu maritus/a?-->are you married?

Sum Maritus/a--> I am married.

Uxorem/maritum Habeo--> I have a wife/husband.

The Romans found a many ways to enjoy their leisure time. One of the most famous ways that the Romans spent their time was to hold gladiatorial contests. The gladiatorial games, wherein men often fought each other to the death, were a violent and bloody entertainment. It is believed that the original gladiatorial games began as a way to honor the dead. For example, Aeneas held games at the funeral of his father where prisoners of war fought to the death. To support this belief it has been noted that most games were put on when an emperor or prominent citizen died.

Most gladiators were prisoners of war, criminals, or slaves. There were some freedmen who became gladiators willingly. There are even some sources that suggest that there were some women gladiators. Romans even started gladiator schools to train fighters.

In addition to enjoying gladiatorial games Romans enjoyed *venationes* or animal hunts. Men called *bestiarii* killed the animals for the spectator's enjoyment. Romans especially loved to see exotic animals in these events. Some kinds were nearly hunted to extinction to sate the Roman's thirst for entertainment.

There were different classes of gladiators that fought against one another. One of the most distinctive was the *retiarius*, a man who would fight with a net, dagger, and a trident. The *murmillo* wore a fish decorated helmet, had a lot of body armor, and had a gladius and long shield for his fighting equipment. *Samites* fought with a long rectangular-shaped shield, short sword. *Thracians*, another popular gladiator type, were heavily armored and had a curved sword. The goal was to make the games more entertaining by pairing up gladiator types in interesting ways. It was popular to pair *Thracians* with *Murmillos*, and putting *Murmillos* and *Rentinarius* together was another popular match up.

When the gladiators entered the arena they saluted the Emperor and said, *"Ave, imperator, morituri te salutant!"* The games would then begin. When one contestant fell to the ground he could raise his hand to ask for mercy. The crowd would let the emperor know with a *pollice verso* (a turned thumb) whether they wanted the gladiator to live. Historians debate over exactly what kind of gesture the thumb made to signal death versus life, but the basic idea remains. The people let their will be known with a hand signal and the emperor would usually follow their will, and order the winner to take the kill or back off.

Phrases you may have heard at a gladiatorial contest:

Ave, imperator, morituri te salutant!	Hail, emperor, we who are about to die salute you!
Occide, verba, ure!	Kill, hit, burn
Quare tam timide incurrit in ferrum?	Why does he run so timidly onto the sword?
Quare parum audacter occidit?	Why does he kill with so little bravery?

Chariot races

One of the most famous scenes in the history of film is the chariot race in *Ben Hur.* The famous movie scene shows both the excitement and danger that Romans must have loved about this sport. Yet, the movies don't always show an incredibly accurate version of historic events, even if they do a good job at capturing their spirit.

Chariot races took place in a circus, the largest of which was called the *circus maximus* located right in the heart of Rome. Capable of seating between 150, 000-250, 000 people the circus was a huge center of entertainment, and it reported to be built during the Roman Republic.

 Most race tracks had starting gates called *carceres* at which the chariots were lined up at before the race started. The host or emperor would drop a white cloth called a *mappa.* At which sight the crowd shouted, the gates were released, and the race began. The charioteer ran the circular track with a long median down the center called a *spina.* On the ends of the *spina* were two columns that marked the turning point called a *meta.* Dolphin shaped counters were used to keep track of the number of laps.

Roman chariot racing was dominated by teams that spectators kept track of through their colors. The original colors were red and white. Blue and green were added later. Yet, people would choose their favorite team and support it ardently. Charioteers often switched teams, as baseball and basketball players do today. Both horses and charioteers had an extremely high chance of injury and death in the sport, but the racers could make a huge amount of money and garner quite a bit of fame.

The driver's clothing was color coded by what team he was driving for. He would also carry a small curved knife so that he could cut himself from the reins if he got caught in them and was being dragged around the arena. Drivers also wore helmets and protective clothing. There were both four-horse and two-horse races. Traditionally, a race consisted of 7 laps, but sometimes this was changed to 5 to allow more races in one day.

Roman Baths

The baths were a part of the typical Roman's everyday routine. Every afternoon before the evening meal Romans would take themselves to the baths to exercise and clean off. Bath buildings were large and beautifully decorated. There was a fee to get in, but sometimes a wealthy patron would pay the fee for everyone to enter. Most Romans had to go to a public bath because they did not have the space or money for their own baths. Only the wealthiest of Romans could afford to have a bath and exercise complex in their own home. The Baths were a very important place to socialize and share information and gossip. The baths were also considered an important part of maintaining health and wellness.

After paying the fee and entering the *apodyterium* was the first stop. A sort of modern day locker room this is where Romans changed out of their clothes. A slave would then take care of your clothing and hang it up for you. There was a separate *apodyterium* for men and women. In addition, women usually bathed in a smaller but separate set of baths. If the bath house was too small for that sometimes men and women would use the facilities at different times of day, the women in the morning and the men in the afternoon.

Most men would then go to the *palestra* an open place for exercise. The routine was to cover oneself in oil to protect from the dirt. Then exercise by playing ball games, lifting weights, or throwing discus. The oil would then be scraped off with a curved instrument called a *strigil*.

Then would come a long series of baths of different temperatures. The routine taken through the baths varied, but there was usually a *tepidarium*, *caldarium*, *frigidarium*.

Tepidarium was the warm room in the baths. The walls and floor were also kept warm with a heating system underneath. Bathers would usually go here to get warmed up before heading to the *Calidarium* so the change in temperature wasn't so dramatic.

Calidarium was a room that was kept very hot and included a hot plunge bath.

Frigidarium was a cool pool that was entered after being in the *calidarium*. Often the room would contain a swimming pool.

Bath complexes often contained more than just pools and changing rooms. They would offer places to eat, libraries, places to sit and read. Many Baths were full of beautiful art and sculptures. Each town usually had a bath even if it was a small one and the bigger cities would have many bath houses open to the public. Often Roman emperors would build bath houses to keep the people happy.

Chapter 23
Famous Thoughts and Quotations

Famous quotations on human nature

Ecce homo	Behold the man
Errare humanum est.	To err is human
Cogito ergo sum.	I think therefore I am
Semper inops quicumque cupit. (claudian)	Whoever desires is always poor.
Dum inter homines sumus, colamus humanitatem.	While we are among humans, let us foster kindness. –Seneca
Dum viviumus, vivamus	While we live, let us live.
Nosce te ipsum	Know theyself
Panem et circenses	Bread and circuses (masses like entertainment)
Nascentes morimur	Even as we are born we begin to die

Famous legal phrases

Ad hoc	To this, improvised
Ad hominem	To the man, personal attack
Cui bono ?	To whom the benefit?
Caveat emptor	Let the buyer beware
Ex post facto	From a thing done after-refers to laws that are retroactive
Habeas corpus	you should have the body, provide evidence
In absentia	In the absence
Persona non grata	Person not pleasing
Ipso facto	By that very fact
Res ipsa loquitur	The matter speaks for itself
Non sequitur	A statement that does not make logical sense
Minimus non curat lex	The law does not care for trivialities.

Famous lines

Alia iacta est (Caesar)	The dice are cast
Ars longa, vita brevis (Seneca)	Art is long, life is brief

Fortes fortuna juvet	Fortune favors the brave
Mens sana in corpore sano	A healthy mind in a healthy body
Quot homines, tot sententiae	There are as many opinions as there are men
Aut disce aut discede	Either learn or discede
Veni, vidi, vici	I came, I saw, I conqured
Ars gratis artis	Art for the sake of art
Vox populi, vox dei	The voice of the people is the voice of god
Sic semper tyrannis	This always to tyrants
Nunc aut numquam	Now or never
Festina lente	Make haste slowly

Latin for the everyday

Magnum opus	Masterpiece
Tempus fugit	Time flies
Sub rosa	do something secretly
Rara avis	Something unusual
Sine cura	an office without responsibility
Sine qua non	Indispensable
Mirabile dictum	Wonderful to say
Lapsus linguae	Slip of the tongue
Pax vobiscum	Peace be with you
Per annum	Per year
Per capita	Per head
Status quo	The existing state of affairs
Vice versa	With the order reversed
Dum spiro, spero	While I breathe, I hope

Military mottos

Semper paratus!	Always prepared (U.S coast guard)
Semper fidelis	Always faithful (U.S. Marines)
Non sibi sed patriae	Not self, but country (U.S. navy)
Si vis pacem, para bellum	If you wish for peace, prepare for war (British royal navy)
Per ardua ad astra	Through adversity to the stars (British royal airforce)
Per mare, per terram	By sea, by land (Royal marine commandos)

Certa cito	Swift and sure (royal signals)
Pergite!	Forward! (Life Guard Regiment *Hussars*-sweden)
Nos nihil effiere non possumus	There is nothing we are not able to do (Norrland Engineer Company) sweden
In arma, caritas	In war, charity (Italian red cross)
Virtus in periculis firmior	Courage is stronger in danger (Regiment of Cuirassiers)

Abbreviations

A.U.C.	Anno Urbis conditae-from the founding of the city
Ibid	Ibidem –in the same place cited
Cf.	Confer—compare
Cp.	Compara-compare
e.g.	exempli gratia --For the sake of example
Et al.	Et alii/aliae and other (persons/authors)
Etc.	Et cetera and other (things)
i.e.	It est--That is
n.b.	Nota bene—note carefully
v.i.	Vide infra—see below
v.s.	Vide supra—see above
S.P.Q.R.	Senatus populousque romanus
Pass	Passim-throughout

Chatper 24
Roman Authors You Should Definitely Read!

Gaius Julius Caesar

Julius Caesar was not only one of Rome's greatest military commanders, but one of its talented writers. He was considered an excellent orator and good writer during his life time. Sadly, the only writings that have survived are his war commentaries. These books were published just after the events in the battlefield transpired so that Caesar could improve his image at home with the Roman people and maintain his influence by reporting his deeds to them regularly. His Gallic Wars have been recommended for centuries to beginning Latin students because his Latin is so clear and direct.

The text of *Commentariorum De Bello Gallico* can be found at The Latin Library for free. I would however say that buying an edited edition with listed vocabulary and grammar commentary would be very helpful for beginning students.

Below are the first several lines of his *De Bello Gallico*, which describes the tribes and geography of the area.

Gallia est omnis divisa in partes tres, quarum unam incolunt Belgae, aliam Aquitani, tertiam qui ipsorum lingua Celtae, nostra Galli appellantur. Hi omnes lingua, institutis, legibus inter se different.

Publius Vergilius Maro (Virgil)

Virgil is one of the greats and his work, T*he Aeneid* is truly outstanding. Written in dactylic hexameter verse it tells the story of the hero Aeneas and his struggle to found Rome. Commissioned by Emperor Augustus himself the poem is considered a national epic and was instantly recognized as a beautiful piece of literature. Medieval audiences came to regard Virgil as a prophetic magician. Sections of his other poem the Ecologues were believed to prophecy the life of Jesus Christ.

The complete Latin text can be found at the Latin Library for free. Though, *Vergil's Aenied, books I-VI* edited by Clyde Pharr is highly recommended to the student reading the Vergil for the first time. I think this is the standard text for high schools and colleges around the country.

Below are the first few lines of the epic poem talking about the fate of Aneas after the Trojan war ended.

Arma virumque cano, Troiae qui primus ab oris

Italiam, fato profugus, Laviniaque venit

litora, multum ille et terris iactatus et alto

vi superum saevae memorem Iunonis ob iram;

multa quoque et bello passus, dum conderet urbem,

inferretque deos Latio, genus unde Latinum,

Albanique patres, atque altae moenia Romae.

Marcus Tullius Cicero

Cicero is another Roman notable for his Latin prose. Another literary giant of the ancient world Cicero was known as a great Roman orator, lawyer, and philosopher. He served as consul and discovered a conspiracy headed by Lucius Sergius Catilina to overthrow the Roman Republic. He delivered four speeches denouncing Catiline and his followers. They were so powerful that they sent Catiline into hiding. These speeches are still considered great works of rhetorical style and often read by classic students. His writing was considered so great and emblematic of good Latin that almost all writing thereafter was compared by the measuring stick of his style.

Today we have 58 speeches written by Cicero out of the 88 that we knew existed at some point. Cicero also wrote extremely influential books on rhetoric and philosophy. He also wrote about law and the Roman Republic. The ages have preserved over 900 of his letters.

All the text of Cicero's works can be found for free at the Latin Library. *O Tempora! O Mores!: Cicero's Catilinarian Orations*, a Student Edition with Historical Essays by Susan Shapiro is a good resource for the beginning Latin student.

Below are the first few lines of the first catilinarian oration.

Quo usque tandem abutere, Catilina, patientia nostra? quam diu etiam furor iste tuus nos eludet? Quem ad finem sese effrenata iactabit audacia?

Publius Ovidius Naso

Ovid was a famous Roman poet. He is most well-known for his work the Metamorphoses, a mythological narrative that recounts myths that involve transformations. His work mentions over 250 different myths in a catalogue style. This work was well loved in the medieval ages and inspired many different works.
Metamorphosis can be found at the Latin Library for free. There is also a beginning Latin textbook called *Latin Via Ovid* that may make his text more accessible to the beginning Latin student interested in his work.

Below are the first few lines of his famous *Metamorphosis*.

 In nova fert animus mutatas dicere formas

corpora; di, coeptis (nam vos mutastis et illas)

adspirate meis primaque ab origine mundi

ad mea perpetuum deducite tempora carmen!

Titus Livius

Livy was a Roman Historian who is best known for writing *ab urbe condita libri* an enormously long history of Rome that told the story of Rome from the very beginning. The books were extremely popular during Livy's lifetime. The long work was 142 books. Today only about 35 books survive--books 1-10, 21-45. The remaining books have summaries of them so we know what topics they covered by not the full text.

The text of Ab Urbe Condita can be found on for free at the Latin Library. Below is the thesis of his Roman history found in the preface to book one.

Sed haec et his similia utcumque animaduersa aut existimata erunt haud in magno equidem ponam discrimine: ad illa mihi pro se quisque acriter intendat animum, quae vita, qui mores fuerint, per quos viros quibusque artibus domi militiaeque et partum et auctum imperium sit; labente deinde paulatim disciplina velut desidentes primo mores sequatur animo, deinde ut magis magisque lapsi sint, tum ire coeperint praecipites, donec ad haec tempora quibus nec vitia nostra nec remedia pati possumus perventum est.

Marcus Valerius Martialis

Martial was a Roman poet famous for his epigrams. Many of which are satirical observations of life around him. His clever and witty style endeared him to many students of Latin. Martial is the father of the modern day epigram and many have tried to imitate his comic style.

The difficulty of Martial's Latin varies from epigram to epigram. They are fun to read and naturally put into bite sized chunks. I don't know of any student texts of Martial, but the text can be found at the Latin Library for free.

32 Non amo te, Sabidi, nec possum dicere quare:

hoc tantum possum dicere, non amo te.

Conclusion
Now Embark on Your Own Adventure!

Congratulations! You have made it to the end of this book and have introduced yourself to quite a few aspects of the Latin language. I hope you have learned some interesting and useful things along the way. I hope you have an appreciation for the beauty of this language. Sometimes I am amazed at how many English words it takes to translate one Latin verb, and occasionally I will wish I could convey my thoughts as succinctly as a Roman could.

So now that you have completed this basic introduction to Latin I must warn you that you have only taken a small step in one long journey. This book did not cover every single nuance of Latin grammar but introduced the reader to the many of the main grammar concepts that are admittedly not always easy to understand.

Then there is the massive amount of rote repetition and memorization that must be undertaken to master verb and noun endings, vocabulary, and grammatical structures. All of this will take time and work, but the more work you put into it he more you will get out of it. It is often easy to link Latin vocabulary to English derivatives to jog your memory. It is also fun to run across phrases and mottos that you have heard in passing and can now analyze with new knowledge. It is also fun to use Latin for everyday greetings—Salvete!—and study. Start writing out those abbreviations et cetera, et cetera, et cetera.

This book didn't cover every aspect of Latin grammar as it was supposed to be a general introduction. So there is more to be learned. There are more uses for the cases than I put in the text, and more uses for the subjunctive. I also didn't tell you how to form every single verb tense so you'll need to learn how to do the future perfect and pluperfect. There are also things like participles, supines, gerunds and gerundives, personal and relative pronouns, demonstrative adjectives, and handful of other small things. I learned my grammar from *Wheelock's Latin* and I would recommend it especially since it focuses on taking its practice sentences directly from Roman writers.

This book isn't going to help if you want to jump immediately into reading original Latin texts. You'll be able to pick phrases out here and there, but reading comprehension comes with acquaintance with the language. The best way to learn to read Latin is to read lots and lots of easy Latin and slowly increase in difficulty. I'd recommend working yourself through a **read to learn** Latin program. There are several really great textbook series that focus on this approach to learning Latin: *Cambridge Latin Course, Ecce Romani, Oxford Latin Course.*

Of course there are also great resources online. My absolute favorite online resource is the William Whittaker's online Latin dictionary. And The Latin Library has many Latin texts online for free. They are easy to print out and easy to find by writer. The Perseus Digital Library also has an electronic version of many Latin books with hyperlinked vocabulary. The website www.nodictionaries.com will generate an automatic vocabulary word list for many popular Roman texts. This is an excellent resource for those that don't want to look up vocabulary for hours, as I did as an undergrad student.

My advice from here is to study hard and have fun!

Valete!

Dagny Taggart

Prologue
Why You Should Learn Greek

Did you ever wonder why you should learn one of the least spoken languages in the world?

Then you should think twice, since it is might spoken by, more or less 12 million people but...

If you are this person that loves archeology and ancient cultures of our planet, then you should definitely visit Greece! It is the land of one of the earliest civilizations of mankind and "every stone you pick, you will find a trace"! Numerous archeological sites and museums are there for you!

Are you keen on philosophy and drama? It is a great chance to explore their paths, but also a great part of many other sciences' evolution, like astronomy, medicine and mathematics. Read the ancient writings on marble that you will meet and even if Antique Greek language turned into Koine Greek and finally to its modern version, try to solve the riddle!

Moreover, heritage of the Ancients Greeks is very rich and, definitely, if you dig deeper into the things nowadays, you will find it! The ancient language of Greece inspired many others. Words "borrowed" to your language can be found, as well as words that Modern Greek language borrowed from yours! Exploring the paths of languages, getting to know them better and even understanding your own native language in a more profound way is a very big advantage in this era that communication is breaking down.

For sure, when visiting a country, you have at least some basic language skills, gives you more opportunities to be better understood and understand better the people around you, how they think and who they are. It is a chance to be appreciated, since people seeing you making efforts to use their "code" and trying to handle it with care will love you at first sight. And who knows? Maybe you will make lifelong friends and acquaintances!

Finally, learning a new language is always a challenge for our brain! It increases our skills of every kind, like cognitive and life ones, plus you can only get happy and satisfied by the novelty of it all and the new roads that will be wide open for you!

So, why not to try it out? You don't need to rush in anything. Try to spell a few words with the first native speaker out there and little – by – little everything mentioned above will come to you!

Important note

Due to the nature of this book (it contains charts, graphs, and so on), you will better your reading experience by setting your device on *LANDSCAPE* mode! (In case you're using a Kindle device).

Let's Set The Right Ground for Learning...

First of all: feel as much confident as possible and think that you only have to break the barriers on your way! There is no place for feeling shy or afraid while learning a new language.

Start using the language whenever you have the chance! For sure you will make mistakes – mistakes are made even in our mother tongue! Do not feel bad about it, nor ashamed. You should even chase the chance to be corrected. By experiencing you will learn!

Try to read and try to write even if the alphabet is different! Read out loud, for better results. Accent is not the aim of this but understanding when someone speaks to you, a fact that allows you to answer to the right thing every time and get involved in longer discussions every time. You can start with children's stories as vocabulary is simplified and this way you can enrich your skills but also not get disappointed in the mid way.

If you like to study, just do it! You can attend classes of any language, theoretically speaking, you can use a little phrasebook during your stay in another land or you can even grab the chance of a summer school at your destination.

Prefer to practice the language with, mostly, native speakers. You will challenge your mind since, usually, they speak faster and they are using idioms and colloquialisms, but this way you will blend in a better and more effective way with the local spirit and you will get more out of it, in less time!

Now, prepare your mind, pack your luggage and embark into this new trip in knowledge, skills and life!

Are you ready?

Let's get started!

SECTION 1: ACQUIRE YOUR BASIC SKILLS!

Chapter 1: The Greek Alphabet and Pronunciation

Learn how to pronounce Greek words.

The Greek Alphabet is a successor of the Phoenician Alphabet that influenced the birth both of the Latin and Cyrillic Alphabet. It consists of 24 letters, 7 vowels and 17 consonants, that combined give us more phonemes, not existing in the original alphabet. Greek is considered to be a *syllable – timed* language, therefore difficulties in reading and accent will not be an issue.

Differences between English and Greek Language

Upper & Lower Case Letter	Greek & English Name	Pronunciation	Example
Α, α	Άλφα/ Alpha	[a]	what
Β, β	Βήτα/ Beta	[v]	visit
Γ, γ	Γάμμα/ Gamma	[γ]	year
Δ, δ	Δέλτα/ Delta	[δ]	there
Ε, ε	Έψιλον/ Epsilon	[e]	after
Ζ, ζ	Ζήτα/ Zeta	[z]	zero
Η, η	Ήτα/ Eta	[i]	begin
Θ, θ	Θήτα/ Theta	[θ]	thing
Ι, ι	Ιώτα/ Iota	[i]	fish
Κ, κ	Κάππα/ Kappa	[k]	take
Λ, λ	Λάμδα/ Lambda	[l]	London
Μ, μ	Μι/ Mu	[m]	moon
Ν, ν	Νι/ Nu	[n]	night
Ξ, ξ	Ξι/ Xi	[ks]	box
Ο, ο	Όμικρον/ Omicron	[o]	olive
Π, π	Πι/ Pi	[p]	pen
Ρ, ρ	Ρω/ Rho	[r]	right
Σ, σ	Σίγμα/ Sigma	[s]	sandal
Τ, τ	Ταυ/ Tau	[t]	tea
Υ, υ	Ύψιλον/ Upsilon	[i]	ink
Φ, φ	Φι/ Phi	[f]	fork
Χ, χ	Χι/ Chi	[χ]	hotel
Ψ, ψ	Ψι/ Psi	[ps]	eclipse
Ω, ω	Ωμέγα/ Omega	[o]	office

Although you will notice similarities, especially in the words and terminology, you can spot differences between English and Greek in almost every feature of them, syntax, morphology, grammar, punctuation, phonetics and phonology.

The syntax in Greek is not as strict as in English, as it always matters what you want to point out of the elements of your sentence. What you put first in the sequence is usually what is more important.

Example:

- Σπουδάζω Οικονομικά.

- Οικονομικά σπουδάζω.

  The meaning of both sentences is *"I'm studying Economics"*. The first sentence follows the regular syntax rule (S-V-O). In the second one object and verb are reversed to emphasize on the object.

So, sequence of the terms can be S-V-O, V-S-O, O-V-S or V-O-S.

You will have noticed that subject is missing in both of them. This is something that also differs between these two languages. You can skip the use of the subject completely, especially the pronouns, since every time it is connoted by the suffix of the verb. This bond between morphology, syntax and grammar can make Greek language seem very perplexed but very charming as a field of study also.

In grammar, it needs to be mentioned that in Greek there are three genders for articles, nouns, adjectives and participles: masculine, feminine and neuter. There are also four cases: nominative, genitive, accusative and vocative and of course, same as in English two numbers: singular and plural. When it comes to verbs, there are three voices: active, passive and middle, two main moods: indicative for all persons, imperative only for the 2nd one of both numbers and subjunctive that is formed directly from the indicative and the word "να" ("na") before it. Fortunately, in tenses there aren't any significant differences, but for every person there is a different suffix.

Regarding punctuation, it is enough to say that the upper score of English (";") is the question mark of Greek and the upper score of Greek is indeed an upper score ("·").

In phonetics and phonology differences are easier to notice. There are numerous phonemes and morphemes to be pronounced that give various sounds that do not exist in English.
Examples:

- Ψάρι [Psari], *fish*
- Ξανά [ksana], *again*

Dipthongs in Greek language.

Diphthong	Pronunciation	Pronunciation before θ/ κ/ ξ/ π/ σ/ τ/ φ/ χ/ ψ	Example
Αι, αι	[e]		Αίγυπτος [Eyiptos]
Ει, ει	[i]		ειρήνη [irini]
Οι, οι	[i]		οικολογία [ikoloyia]
Υι, υι	[yi]		υιοθετώ [yiotheto]
Ου, ου	[u]		ουρανός [uranos]
Αυ, αυ	[av]	[af]	αύρα [avra], αυτί [afti]
Ευ, ευ	[ev]	[ef]	Ευρώπη [Evropi], ευχαριστώ [efharisto]
Μπ, μπ	[b]		μπύρα [bira]
Ντ, ντ	[d]		ντουλάπι [dulapi]
Τζ, τζ	[dz]		Τζατζίκι [dzadziki]
Τσ, τσ	[ts]		τσιγάρο [tsiyaro]
Γκ, γκ	[g], [ng]		Ελ Γκρέκο [El

			Greko]
Γγ, γγ	[g], [ng]		αγγελία [agelia]
Γχ, γχ	[nχ]		άγχος [anχos]

The stress in Greek Language

In Modern Greek language there is only one stress, in one of the last three syllables. The syllable that carries the stress is of longer amplitude and duration. Mind that monosyllabic words do not carry the stress.

Exercises:

1) Transcribe the following words.
- Σπίτι (*house*)
- Αεροπλάνο (*airplane*)
- Ταξίδι (*trip*)
- Οικογένεια (*family*)
- Κείμενο (*text*)
- Κουνούπι (*mosquito*)
- Ευτυχία (*happiness*)

2) Match the word with its pronunciation

μιλάω	thélo
θέλω	ksílo
σκύλος	máska
βίντεο	tsáda
ξύλο	vídeo
μάσκα	miláo
τσάντα	skílos

3) Try to read out loud the sentences, emphasizing in the highlighted syllables

- Πέρυσι το καλοκαίρι, πήγα για διακοπές στην Ελλάδα.
  Pérysi to kalokéri, píga gia diakopés stin Elláda.
  Last summer I went on holiday in Greece.

- Είμαι τριάντα χρονών.
  Íme triánta chronón.
  I am thirty years old.

- Κάνει ζέστη.
  Káni zésti.
  It's hot.

"Loan Words" in Greek and words that Greek loaned

Greek language, on her way through the centuries and up to now, carried along the so – called "loan words". These are words that were adopted by other languages and cultures, English language included, especially in technology, economics, sociology, art and sports' terminology.

Examples:

- σκορ/ score, κάμερα/ camera, τούνελ/ tunnel, χιούμορ/ humour, μιούζικαλ/ musical etc.
-

On the other hand, many words were imported in English, either directly from Greek, or via Latin and its descendants. The presence of Greek is more vivid in scientific terminology.
Examples:

- telephone/ τηλέφωνο, paradise/ παράδεισος, physics/ φυσική, climate/ κλίμα, diagnosis/ διάγνωση, energy/ ενέργεια etc.

Chapter 1: Answers of the exercises

1) Spiti, aeroplano, taksidi, ikogenia, kimeno, koonoopi, eftixia.

2) Μιλάω – milao, θέλω – thelo, σκύλος – skilos, βίντεο – video, ξύλο – ksilo, μάσκα – maska, τσάντα - tsanta

The definite article and its cases

	Masculine	Feminine	Neuter
Nominative	o [o]	η [i]	το [to]
Genitive	του [too]	της [tis]	του [too]
Accusative	τον [ton]	την [tin]	το [to]
Nominative	οι [i]	οι [i]	τα [ta]
Genitive	των [ton]	των [ton]	των [ton]
Accusative	τους [toos]	τις [tis]	τα [ta]

The indefinite article and its cases

	Masculine	Feminine	Neuter
Nominative	ένας [enas]	μια [mia]	ένα [ena]
Genitive	ενός [enos]	μιας [mias]	ενός [enos]
Accusative	έναν [enan]	μια [mia]	ένα [ena]

In Greek, articles agree with the noun that they characterize, regarding gender, number and case. The definite article is always used, whether the indefinite one can be avoided.

Personal Pronouns

	1st person	2nd person	3rd person
Nominative	εγώ [ego]	εσύ [esi]	Αυτός, τος/ αυτή, τη/ αυτό, το [aftos], [tos]/ [afti], [ti]/ [afto], [to]
Genitive	εμένα, μου [emena], [moo]	εσένα, σου [esena], [soo]	Αυτού, του/ αυτής, της/ αυτού, του [aftoo], [too]/ [aftis], [tis]/ [aftoo], [too]
Accusative	εμένα, με [emena], [me]	εσένα, σε [esena], [se]	Αυτόν, τον/ αυτήν, την/ αυτό, το [afton], [ton]/ [aftin], [tin]/

			[afto], [to]
Nominative	εμείς [emis]	εσείς [esis]	αυτοί, τοι/ αυτές, τες/ αυτά, τα [afti], [ti]/ [aftes], [tes]/ [afta], [ta]
Genitive	εμάς, μας [emas], [mas]	εσάς, σας [esas], [sas]	Αυτών, των [afton], [ton]
Accusative	εμάς, μας [emas], [mas]	εσάς, σας [esas], [sas]	αυτοί, τοι/ αυτές, τες/ αυτά, τα [afti], [ti]/ [aftes], [tes]/ [afta], [ta]

Pronouns in Greek have got two types: the strong one and the weak one. The weak type is mostly used in the accusative case, as the object of the sentence, instead of the strong type.

Examples:

- Τον είδα. *I saw him.*
  instead of
  Είδα αυτόν.

- Σε πήρα τηλέφωνο. *I called you.*
  instead of
  Πήρα εσένα τηλέφωνο.

- Μου δάνεισε ένα βιβλίο. *(She) borrowed me one book.*
  instead of
  Δάνεισε σε εμένα ένα βιβλίο.

To be, to do and to have.

	To be	To do	To have
Εγώ	Είμαι [ime]	Κάνω [kano]	Έχω [eχo]
Εσύ	Είσαι [ise]	Κάνεις [kanis]	Έχεις [eχeis]

Αυτός –	Είναι	Κάνει	Έχει
Αυτή –	[ine]	[kani]	[eχi]
Αυτό			
Εμείς	Είμαστε	Κάνουμε	Έχουμε
	[imaste]	[kanoome]	[eχoome]
Εσείς	Είστε	Κάνετε	Έχετε
	[iste]	[kanete]	[eχete]
Αυτοί -	Είναι	Κάνουν	Έχουν
Αυτές-	[ine]	[kanoon]	[eχoon]
Αυτά			

Question words

To form a question, using a question word, in Greek you do it just as in English.
First goes the question word and then the verb, plus the object if there is any and at last you put the question mark ";".

The most common question words in Greek are:

Πόσος/ πόση/ πόσο; [posos]/ [posi]/ [poso] How+adj. (masculine/ feminine/ neuter)?	Ποιος/ ποια/ ποιο; [pios]/ [pia]/ [pio] Who (masculine/ feminine)/ which?	Τι; [ti] What?	Πώς; [pos] How?
Πού; [poo] Where?	Πότε; [pote] When?	Γιατί; [yiati] Why?	Πόσο; [poso] How much?

Examples:

- Που είναι το μετρό; [Poo ine to metro?] (*Where is the metro?*)

- Γιατί κλαις; [Yiati kles?] (*Why are you crying?*)

- Πώς σε λένε; [Pos se lene?] (*What's your name?*)

- Πότε θα έρθεις; [Pote tha erthis?] (*When are you coming?*)

- Τι θα θέλατε; [Ti tha thelate?] (*What would you like?, pl.*)

Meet the numbers!

Learning and memorizing the numbers is not going to be difficult since same rules that apply in English, apply also in Greek.

Numbers from zero to twenty are unique and then all you have to do is to combine!

- From zero to twenty.

0 Μηδέν [miden]	7 Επτά [epta]	14 Δεκατέσσερα [dekatessera]
1 Ένα [ena]	8 Οκτώ [okto]	15 Δεκαπέντε [dekapente]
2 Δύο [dyo]	9 Εννέα [ennea]	16 Δεκαέξι [dekaeksi]
3 Τρία [tria]	10 Δέκα [deka]	17 Δεκαεπτά [dekaepta]
4 Τέσσερα [tessera]	11 Έντεκα [enteka]	18 Δεκαοκτώ [dekaokto]
5 Πέντε [pente]	12 Δώδεκα [dodeka]	19 Δεκαεννιά [dekaennia]
6 Έξι [eksi]	13 Δεκατρία [dekatria]	20 Είκοσι [ikosi]

- Thirty, forty … to one hundred.

30 τριάντα [trianta]	40 σαράντα [saranta]	50 πενήντα [peninta]	60 εξήντα [eksinta]
70 εβδομήντα	80 ογδόντα	90 ενενήντα	100 εκατό

[evdominta]   [ogdonta]   [eneninta]   [ekato]

- Two hundred and more…

200/ διακόσια [diakosia]	300/ τριακόσια [triakosia]	400/ τετρακόσια [tetrakosia]	500/ πεντακόσια [pentakosia]	600/ εξακόσια [eksakosia]
700/ επτακόσια [eptakosia]	800/ οκτακόσια [oktakosia]	900/ εννιακόσια [eniakosia]	1.000/ χίλια [xilia]	1.000.000/ ένα εκατομμύριο [ena ekatomyrio]

:… and what about forming numbers?

✓ 20 is είκοσι [ikosi]. In order to form 25 you put together είκοσι and πέντε (είκοσι πέντε), for 26 you need again είκοσι and έξι (είκοσι έξι) etc.

✓ 100 is εκατό [ekato]. To form 137, you combine εκατό and τριάντα επτά (εκατόν τριάντα επτά), for 193 you need εκατό, ενενήντα and τρία (εκατόν ενενήντα τρία) etc.

✓ For 1.000 and more, all you need is to do the same thing but use χίλια [xilia] before everything and for 2.000 and more use "χιλιάδες" [xiliades] (*thousands*) instead of "χίλια" (*one thousand*).

✓ Respectively, 1.000.000 is ένα εκατομμύριο [ena ekatomyrio] and for 2.000.000 and more the word εκατομμύριο becomes εκατομμύρια [ekatomyria], e.g. δύο εκατομμύρια, τρία εκατομμύρια.

- The ordinal numbers.

1st πρώτος	2nd δεύτερος	3rd τρίτος [tritos]	4th τέταρτος	5th πέμπτος [pemptos]

[protos]	[defteros]		[tetartos]	
6ᵗʰ έκτος	7ᵗʰ έβδομος	8ᵗʰ	9ᵗʰ ένατος	10ᵗʰ
[ektos]	[evdomos]	όγδοος	[enatos]	δέκατος
		[ogdoos]		[dekatos]

✓ Since they are used as adjectives, they are formed in the three genders that exist in Greek and they are used in all the cases, using the suffix that needs to be put every time: πρώτος – πρώτη – πρώτο, δεύτερος – δεύτερη – δεύτερο etc.

The colors

Τι χρώμα είναι ο/ η/ το;

[ti χroma ine o/ i/to]

What color is the … ?

Άσπρο or Λευκό stands for white

Μαύρο stands for black.

Γκρι stands for grey.

Κόκκινο stands for red.

Πράσινο stands for green.

Κίτρινο stands for yellow.

Μπλε stands for blue and γαλάζιο for light blue.

καφέ stands for brown.

πορτοκαλί stands for orange.

Ροζ stands for pink.

Μωβ stands for purple.

Some words that you will use really often

Ναι [ne]
is "yes"

Όχι [οχi]
is "no"

Εντάξει [entaksi]
is "OK"

Και [ke]
is "and"

Ευχαριστώ
[efharisto]
is "Thank you"

Παρακαλώ
[parakalo]
is "You're welcome"

Συγγνώμη
[sygnomi]
is "Sorry"

Σε παρακαλώ
[se parakalo] for 1 person
or
Σας παρακαλώ for more people
is "Please"

Exercises:

1) Rewrite the noun with the correct article.

   - Πατέρας (Father) →
   - Μητέρα (Mother) →
   - Σπίτι (House) →
   - Μάθημα (Lesson) →
   - Δουλειά (Work) →
   - Καιρός (Weather) →
   - Αυτοκίνητο (Car) →
   - Θέατρο (Theatre) →
   - Βιβλίο (Book) →

2) Find the right pronoun for each verb.

   - Κάνουμε μπάνιο στην θάλασσα. →

   - Είμαι από την Αγγλία. →

      - Είμαστε διακοπές. →

      - Τι κάνετε; →

      - Έχεις ένα στυλό; →

- o   Είναι 3 χρονών. →

3) In each sentence there is one weak type of a pronoun. Could you find the strong one?

- o   Μας έδωσαν λίγο γλυκό. (*They gave us some sweet*) →

- o   Τους πήρα τηλέφωνο. (*I called them*) →

- o   Την είδα στο σούπερ – μάρκετ. (*I saw her at the super market*)→

- o   Σου είπα την αλήθεια. (*I told you the truth*)→

- o   Με λένε Δημήτρη. (*My name is Dimitris*)→

4) Write the numbers in Greek.
- o   26 →
- o   83 →
- o   99 →
- o   152 →
- o   866 →
- o   365 →
- o   1.560 →
- o   3.220 →
- o   7.790 →
- o   1.000.400 →
- o   2.350.000 →
- o   7.670.200 →

5) Translate the following sentences:

- o   Το αυτοκίνητο είναι κόκκινο

- o   Κάνω μάθημα ελληνικών.

- o   Είμαι είκοσι έξι χρονών.

- o   Η μητέρα είναι στο σπίτι.

o   Έχω δέκα βιβλία.

Chapter 2: Answers of the exercises

1) Ο πατέρας, η μητέρα, το σπίτι, το μάθημα, η δουλειά, ο καιρός, το αυτοκίνητο, το θέατρο, το βιβλίο.

2) Εμείς, εγώ, εμείς, εσείς, εσύ, αυτός/ αυτή/ αυτό

3) Εμάς, αυτούς, αυτήν, εσένα, εμένα.

4) Είκοσι έξι, ογδόντα τρία, ενενήντα εννιά, εκατόν πενήντα δύο, οκτακόσια εξήντα έξι, τριακόσια εξήντα πέντε, χίλια πεντακόσια εξήντα, τρεις χιλιάδες διακόσια είκοσι, επτά χιλιάδες επτακόσια ενενήντα, ένα εκατομμύριο τετρακόσια, δύο εκατομμύρια τριακόσιες πενήντα χιλιάδες, επτά εκατομμύρια εξακόσια εβδομήντα διακόσια.

5) Το αυτοκίνητο είναι κόκκινο = the car is red, Κάνω μάθημα ελληνικών = I am taking classes of Greek, Είμαι είκοσι έξι χρονών = I am 26 years old, Η μητέρα είναι στο σπίτι = Mother is at home, Έχω δέκα βιβλία = I've got ten books.

To check out the rest of "Learn Greek In 7 DAYS! - The Ultimate Crash Course to Learning the Basics of the Greek Language In No Time" go to Amazon and look for it right now!

Ps: You'll find many more books like these under my name, Dagny Taggart. Don't miss them! Here's a short list:

- Learn **Spanish** In 7 Days!
- Learn **French** In 7 Days!
- Learn **German** In 7 Days!
- Learn **Italian** In 7 Days!
- Learn **Portuguese** In 7 Days!

- Learn **Japanese** In 7 Days!
- Learn **Chinese** In 7 Days!

- Learn **Russian** In 7 Days!

- Learn Any Language FAST!

- How to Drop *Everything* & Travel Around The World

About the Author

Dagny Taggart is a language enthusiast and polyglot who travels the world, inevitably picking up more and more languages along the way.

Taggart's true passion became learning languages after she realized the incredible connections with people that it fostered. Now she just can't get enough of it. Although it's taken time, she has acquired vast knowledge on the best and fastest ways to learn languages. But the truth is, she is driven simply by her motive to build exceptional links and bonds with others.

She is inspired everyday by the individuals she meets across the globe. For her, there's simply not anything as rewarding as practicing languages with others because she gets to make friends with people from all that come from a variety of cultures. This, in turn, has broadened her mind and thinking more than she would have ever imagined it could.

Of course, as a result of her constant travels, Taggart has become an expert on planning trips and making the most of time spent out of what she calls her "base" town. She jokes that she's practically at the nomad status now, but she's more content to live that way.

She knows how to live on a manageable budget weather she's in Paris or Phnom Penh. She knows how to seek out the adventures and thrills, no doubt, lying in wait at any city she visits. She knows that reflection on each every experience is significant if she wants to grow as a traveler and student of the world's cultures.

Because of this, Taggart chooses to share her understanding of languages and travel so that others, too, can experience the same life-altering benefits she has.

Printed in Great Britain
by Amazon.co.uk, Ltd.,
Marston Gate.